This OPUS edition, published in 1988, is an unabridged and unaltered re-publication of the work originally published by Russell Odiorne, Boston, Massachusetts, 1833.

Library of Congress Cataloging-in-Publication Data

Breck, Joseph, 1794-1873.
   The young florist, or, Conversations on the culture of flowers, and on natural history.

   Reprint. Originally published: Boston : Russell, Odiorne, 1833.
   Includes index.
   Summary: An ongoing dialogue between two young gardeners introduces information about flowers and natural history as it relates to the cultivation of a flower garden.
   1. Flower gardening — Juvenile literature.   2. Natural history — Juvenile literature.   [1. Flower gardening.   2. Gardening.   3. Natural history] I. Title.   II.Title: Young Florist.   III. Title: Conversations on the culture of flowers and on natural history.
SB406.5.B74   1988   635.9   87-31444
ISBN 0-940983-20-6

Manufactured in the United States of America on "acid-free' stock.

OPUS Publications, Inc., Post Rd. P.O. Box 269
Guilford, Connecticut 06437

America Blossoms

"Let every home if possible be accompanied with the pleasures . . . of a well-kept garden," one nineteenth century author wrote listing "the climbing vine, the swelling bud, the opening blossom (and) the glowing beauty of nature's coloring."

Joseph Breck's first book was written as a dialogue for children describing a garden plan and the plants to create the desired effect both horizontally and vertically for maximum pleasure. The plan has been adapted for the garden of the Fitch House at Old Sturbridge Village as part of the re-creation of daily life in rural New England in the first half of the nineteenth century.

Write to the Village for a free calendar of events.

Old Sturbridge Village
1 Old Sturbridge Village Road
Sturbridge, MA 01566

OPUS Publications, Inc., Post Road Box 269
Guilford, CT 06437

See page 8.

THE

YOUNG FLORIST;

OR

CONVERSATIONS

ON

THE CULTURE OF FLOWERS,

AND ON

NATURAL HISTORY,

WITH NUMEROUS ENGRAVINGS, FROM ORIGINAL DESIGNS.

BY JOSEPH BRECK,

Superintendent of the Horticultural Garden, Lancaster, Mass.

BOSTON:

RUSSELL, ODIORNE AND CO.

1833.

BOSTON:
PRINTED BY TUTTLE AND WEEKS.

PREFACE.

———

THIS work is designed by the author to attract young persons to that delightful employment, the cultivation of a flower garden. It consists of familiar dialogues between the juvenile cultivators; the scenes of which are laid in the garden and the fields, so as to impart reality and animation to their inquiries. With the study of flowers he has endeavored to intermingle a taste for natural history, by introducing many incidental facts relative to insects, &c. that naturally suggest themselves in the culture of a garden. How well he has succeeded, the public must judge.

THE YOUNG FLORIST.

MARCH.

Margaret. O, Henry, pray come to the door and hear this sweet bird, how delightfully he sings.

Henry. Yes, dear sister, his notes are cheering indeed; it is the blue bird, see! there he flies.

M. What broad and full wings he has, and how beautifully the rich azure blue of his back is contrasted with the rusty iron color of his breast and the white beneath. He seems to say, how grateful I am for this fine morning.

H. This beautiful morning, and the tones of the blue bird, tell us that winter is nearly over, and that spring is approaching, decked with a profusion of flowers.

M. How glad I shall be, after so much snow and ice and cold, to have warm weather come, the green grass spring up, and the little flowers appear; and then our Crocuses and Snow Drops will be first to cheer the desolation of the garden.

H. Get your hat and cloak, and we will take a trip over the fields, on the hard crust of snow, and talk of a plan for a new garden I have in my mind, as you know we have but a small patch, which was so crowded with plants last year that it looked like a thicket.

M. With all my heart, dear brother; the thought of again resuming our labors in the garden, this fine morning, and your company will make a walk very grateful.

H. Take my arm, and we will cross the brook over the log bridge, and pass through the woodland where we built our rustic arbor last season, to the hill where we have so often enjoyed ourselves in gathering wild flowers, and making them into garlands, under the shade of the beautiful clump of trees that adorn its brow.

M. Now for your plan, which is uppermost in my mind.

H. You always seem to be pleased with flowers and the operations of the garden ; and it seems strange to me that any person can be insensible to the profusion of beauty, which God, in his infinite goodness, has seen fit to bestow upon flowers. The great variety of colors and shades, shapes and odors, which meets our eyes and perfumes the air, at every step we take, should lead our admiring souls up to the great Creator of all things, who seems to smile in every flower we see.

M. I have often thought, some of my most

2

pleasant hours have been spent in the garden;
how calm and happy I have been, when rising
early from my bed, to observe the progress of
the plants, while my ears were greeted with
the softest music from every shrub and tree;
and if ever my soul has been filled with love
and gratitude to our Heavenly Father, it was
then.

H. While we are engaged in the garden,
we are not confined altogether to flowers;
for we see a multitude of other objects which
attract our attention, such as birds and insects,
and we shall be led to study the history of
these, which will interest us more and more
at every step we take; so that while our bodies
are benefited by the healthy exercise we take,
our minds will be more expanded, and our views
more enlarged, and it is on this account that
our dear father has promised us a larger piece
of ground, on which we may enjoy ourselves,
when not engaged in study or other duties.

M. Do tell me where it is.

H. At the bottom of the garden, on the brook that so gracefully winds through the meadow below.

M. What, by the great elm?

H. Yes; you know it was cultivated last year and is now in good order; and father will let Daniel do some of the hardest work, such as wheeling gravel for the walks.

M. He is a kind father; he is always ready to do anything which he knows will be for our good. What a delightful spot this is; so high above the brook that it will always be free from wet; and then its banks you know are lined with some fine native shrubs, which will be quite an acquisition to the garden.

H. There is the bunch of Kalmia that we have so often admired with its evergreen, shining leaves, and showy pink flowers, which Daniel was going to cut down; he said it was

Kill Lamb, and would poison the sheep; I prevented him and told him we did not pasture our sheep in the garden.

M.   And then there is my favorite, the Wild Rose, so delicious and fragrant; the Rodora, whose beautiful purple blossoms appear so early, even before the leaf buds begin to unfold; the Azalea or Swamp Honeysuckle, whose flowers perfume the air in June; and the Black Alder, with its fine scarlet berries, which so enlivens the autumnal scenery.

H.   We will have a fine collection of American plants; these we have named; and many others are among the most ornamental that can be brought from any country; we will at our leisure search the woods, meadows and fields for flowers and plants to decorate our little patch, and although we can afford to buy but a few plants, we will have a garden the gayest of the gay.

M. The Violets and other wild flowers we transplanted last year have done wonderfully, and will encourage us to go on until we have all our native plants within the compass of a few yards. But how do you mean to lay out the ground?

H. I have a plan in view, but should like first to know what your taste is.

M. I am of opinion it should not be laid out too mechanically — I am pleased with serpentine walks and irregular plats or beds. We should strive to imitate nature as much as possible, which has a much better effect than a stiff formality ; and as a proof of this, do but notice this beautiful winding pathway, through the grove in which we are now walking, and compare it with the straight one which we have just left, and say if this does not give greater pleasure to the eye?

H. Your taste is very good ; but remember

ours would be but a puny imitation of nature, in a garden forty feet square; had we acres of pleasure ground, I should admire to lay it out in the style you suggest.

M. Now I remember you are studying geometry, and of course you will want to mark it out with the square and compasses; but I feel quite satisfied to submit entirely to your superior judgment. What is your plan?

H. I have been contriving one, but can explain it to you better on paper than in any other way, and will show it to you this evening.

M. Do. I am impatient to see it, but it is time to return; I am afraid we shall be late at school, and the bright warm sun begins to soften the snow; a few days more and the snow banks which are so piled up beside the walls, and make the passage of them so easy, will disappear.

H. Yes, but we shall have much boisterous weather yet, as this is only the 4th of March, and winter and spring will have many a hard encounter, before the latter comes off conqueror.

M. We were so delighted with the appearance of the blue bird this morning that I have a mind to note it down in our floral calendar.

When evening came, Henry produced the plan, which you see on the preceding page. It was altogether unintelligible to Margaret until he explained it in the following manner.

H. You see here a square, within which are three circular beds, or concentric circles, having two rows of figures in each. Now these circles are to be filled with annual flowers, and each number represents a different sort, and you see they are numbered as high as 100, so that I have designed it for one hundred different kinds.

I shall shortly show you a list of these, with their numbers opposite to their respective names.

I have contrived it so that the tallest plants shall be in the centre and cover an arbor, as you see I have marked. You see a walk from the outside of the square to the arbor, communicating with one large and two smaller circular ones.

For the inner circle of all, such plants as climb to the height of ten feet or more, as the Morning Glory, Flowering Beans, &c., for which it will be necessary to put down birch poles with the branches of the tops left on to form the arbor.

For the second row you will find I have selected Sweet Peas, Cypress Vine, Nasturtium, &c. which are also climbers, and will require brush for their support, neatly trimmed, about four and a half feet high.

For the third circular row, the tallest plants which do not climb; and each successive circle of plants diminishes in height to the outer one, which is composed of dwarfs — and you will find by inspecting the key that no two kinds or colors of flowers come together, so that when it is all in bloom, it will have the appearance of a cone of flowers of every shape, color and shade tastefully intermingled, as represented in the following drawing; in which, how-

ever, I have not introduced any arbor, which can be done or not, at pleasure.

M. This will be beautiful, surely, and must have taken some time and patience to arrange it; but I think it will be a perplexing piece of work to transfer it to the ground, and have all the plants sowed in the place you have allotted them.

H. Nothing will be easier, as you will see when I come to lay it out and sow them.

M. What is to be put in the outer part of the figure, and what is the meaning of the letters?

H. That is the place for the perennial plants that we have in our little garden, and for such as we may procure from other gardens and the fields, and may be arranged in any fanciful manner we please. The letters represent fanciful groups of flowers to be in bloom at the same time, for different months of the year, to be composed of annuals and perennials. Ju. for July, Au. for August, A. for

April, M. for May, &c., and here you may have opportunity to exercise your taste.

M. That will please me ; and by the time you get the ground in readiness, I will exhibit a plan for every month in the season.

I wish you would give me a copy of that part which contains the annuals, as I wish to send it to cousin Eliza ; she has but a small piece of ground and her father has no place of his own, and of course does not want to be at the expense of cultivating many perennials, as he moves so often from one place to another.

H. I shall be happy to furnish you with a copy for her, and will also send her a portion of our seeds, with directions how to cultivate them. On the following pages you will see a list of the plants arranged in order ; you will find some numbers and plants inserted twice ; this is done to fill out the circle ; and some of them are very showy. Be particular not to make any mistake while you write it off for her.

A KEY TO THE PLAN FOR A GARDEN.

FIRST CIRCLE.

No.

1	Scarlet Flowering Bean,	scarlet.
‡2	Blue Morning Glory,	dark and light blue.
3	White Flowering Bean	white.
‡4	Rose Morning Glory	purplish red.
5	Purple Flowering Bean	purple.
‡6	Superb Striped Morning Glory	white striped.
‡7	Scarlet Morning Glory, or Ipomea	scarlet.
8	Two Colored Lemon Gourd (*ornamental fruit*) }	yellow.
‡9	Starry Ipomea	delicate blue

SECOND CIRCLE.

‡10	Nasturtium	deep orange.
*11	Scarlet Sweet Pea	red.
‡12	Balloon Vine	white, curious seed pods.
*13	Purple Sweet Pea	purple.
*14	Mexican Ximenisia	yellow.
15	Cypress Vine	brilliant crimson.
*16	White Sweet Pea	white.
‡10	Nasturtium	deep orange.
*17	Tangiers Crimson Sweet Pea	dark crimson.
‡12	Balloon Vine	white.
15	Cypress Vine (*scald this seed*)	crimson.

Third Circle.

‡18	Red Four o'Clock	deep red.
‡19	Violet Zinnia	violet.
‡20	Yellow Immortal Flower	brilliant yellow.
†21	White Chrysanthemum	white.
†22	Prince's Feather	very dark red.
*23	Tall Blue Larkspur	lively blue.
‡24	Yellow Four o'Clock	yellow.
*25	Variegated Euphorbia	elegantly variegated white and green.
†26	Red Lavatera	light red strip'd with deep
‡27	Blue Commelina	celestial blue.
†28	Yellow Chrysanthemum	yellow.
†29	White Lavatera	pure white.
†30	Love Lies Bleeding	blood red.
19	Violet Zinnia	violet.
‡20	Yellow Immortal Flower	brilliant yellow
*21	Variegated Euphorbia	white and green.
†26	Red Lavatera	light red.

Fourth Circle.

†31	Grand Flowering Argemone	elegant white flower and yellow centre.
‡32	Yellow Zinnia	tawny yellow.
*33	American Centaurea	pale purple.
†34	Tricolored Amaranthus	each leaf red, yellow and brown.
‡35	Long Flowered Four o'Clock	white with purple centre.
†36	Grand Flowering Evening Primrose	yellow.

37 Purple Amaranthus
  (Soak the seed in milk 24 hours) } purple.

‡38 Red Zinnia   red.

39 White Amaranthus
  (Soak the seed in milk 24 hours) } white.

*40 Golden Coreopsis   { fine yellow with brown centre.

‡41 Red Opium Poppy   purplish red.

‡42 Crimson Cockscomb   deep crimson.

‡35 Long Flowered Four o'Clock   white with purple.

‡43 African Marigold   orange.

37 Purple Amaranthus   purple.

34 Tricolored Amaranthus   yellow, red and brown.

39 White Amaranthus   white.

‡44 French Marigold   brown velvet orange.

‡41 Red Opium Poppy   purplish red.

‡42 Crimson Cockscomb   deep crimson.

*45 African Hibiscus   { light straw with purple centre.

†46 Night Flowering Primrose   yellow.

‡27 Commelina   bright blue.

FIFTH CIRCLE.

†47 Tricolored Chrysanthemum   white, yellow and brown.

48 D'ble white and variegated Balsams   white and variegated.

†49 Fennel Flower or Love in a Mist   blue.

*50 Red Quilled Aster   red.

†51 Long Flowered Evening Primrose   yellow.

*52 White Expanded Aster   white.

‡53 Blue Lupin   blue.

‡54	Double Carnation Poppy, of sorts	red, pink, &c.
*55	Yellow Hawkweed or Crepis Barbata	yellow and brown.
*56	White Quilled Aster	white.
*57	Blue Bottle	blue.
58	Fire Colored and Crimson Balsams	red.
†59	Scorzonera	deep yellow and brown.
‡60	Double White Fringed Poppy	pure white.
*61	Purple and Lilac expanded Aster	purple and lilac.
†62	Scarlet Malope	red, with purplish stripe.
†63	Pot Marigold	orange.
†64	White Catchfly	white.
‡65	Lemon Balm	blue, and fine scent.
†66	African Rose	every shade of red.
*67	Beautiful Ketmia	straw and purple.
*68	Variegated Asters	{ white, with blue and red stripes.
†69	Azure Blue Gilia	fine blue.
*70	Red Quilled Aster	red.
*45	African Hibiscus	straw and deep purple.
‡71	Sweet Basil, or Lavender	{ white, with delightful scent.
‡72	Mexican Ageratum	blue.
‡73	Double Purple Balsams	purple.
†66	African Rose	every shade of red.
*55	Yellow Hawkweed	yellow and brown.
‡60	White Fringed Poppy	pure white.
†69	Azure Blue Gilia	blue

SIXTH CIRCLE.

*74 Convolvulus Minor	fine blue and yellow.
‡75 Scarlet Cacalia	scarlet.
*76 Snails	yellow, with curious pod.
†77 Sweet Alyssum	white, sweet scented.
*78 Purple Candytuft	purple.
†79 Daisy Leaved Catchfly	fine pink.
*80 Caterpillars	yellow, with curious pod.
†81 White Evening Primrose	pure white.
*82 Double Dwarf Larkspur	purple, pink and white.
†83 Lobel's Catchfly	red.
†84 Mignonette	yellowish, very fragrant.
†85 White Candytuft	white.
‡86 Purple Immortal Flower	fine light purple.
*87 Beautiful Clarkea	red.
*88 Horns	yellow, curious pod.
†89 Venus' Looking Glass	blue.
†90 Red Hawkweed	pale red.
*91 Hedgehogs	yellow, curious pod.
*74 Convolvulus Minor	{ fine blue and yellow centre.
‡75 Scarlet Cacalia	fine scarlet.
†84 Mignonette	yellowish, very fragrant.
†77 Sweet Alyssum	white and fragrant.
‡92 Wing Leaved Schizanthus	{ light and dark, purple and yellow.
93 Sensitive Plant	pink, very curious plant.
*94 Coronilla	beautiful leaf, yellow.
95 Ice Plant	curious plant, white.

†96 Nolana	light and dark blue.
†83 Lobel's Catchfly	red.
†84 Mignonette	yellowish, fragrant.
†81 White Evening Primrose	white.
*97 Forget-me-not	blue.
†79 Daisy Leaved Catchfly	fine pink.
‡98 Thunbergia	fine new plant — yellow and brown.
*99 Heart's Ease	purple, yellow and white.
*87 Beautiful Clarkea	red.
‡100 Purple Jacobea	purple.

A few weeks passed on, during which time Henry was anxiously watching the conflict between winter and spring, now cheered with an almost summer day, then flying for shelter from the rude blasts of winter; and Margaret would occasionally, when the weather was inviting, take a run in the garden to look at the Tulips and Narcissuses, whose foliage was beginning to emerge from their frozen beds, to gather a few blossoms of Heart's Ease, and to hear the notes of the blue bird and sparrow, who seemed to proclaim the speedy approach of spring.

In the meantime Henry prepared his number sticks, which he did in the following manner. Having procured some refuse shingles, he split them into strips an inch wide, and sharpening the thin end, smoothed one side of the other end with his jack-knife ; and then with a small brush rubbed some white lead paint on the smooth side, and with his black lead pencil wrote the number upon the paint and laid them away to dry. — The number thus written will last as long as the stick.

His flower seeds, which had been neatly done up in paper bags and wrote upon as they were gathered, were marked with the number set against their respective names in the catalogue given, and laid away against the time of need.

He had provided himself with a line and made a neat reel to wind it on, also a pole ten feet long, with the feet marked upon it ; and saw that all his tools were in order and ready for use.

APRIL.

At length April was ushered in with a most charming day; thousands of pigeons were seen in successive flocks on their rapid flight; and the robin had taken possession of the uppermost branch of the elm, and was pouring forth his sweet music in delightful strains.

Henry, impatient to commence his operations, applied to his father for Daniel's assistance, which was readily granted.

And now in company with Margaret, with exhilarating feelings, and bounding step, they proceeded to the place allotted them to lay out the long talked of garden; the spot had been

well manured and finely dug and raked smooth-
ly a few days before.

Margaret was to hold the plan while Henry
transferred it to the ground, and Daniel was
directed to dig some turf and cut it into strips
three inches wide to make an edging to the
walks, and also to cut from the woodland near
by, nine birch poles and brush for the climbing
plants.

This he did not do without first giving it as
his opinion, that the land had better be im-
proved in raising potatoes as it was last year,
than to spend so much time and labor about
trifles, from which there was no profit.

But the children knew what a rich harvest
of pleasure they should reap, and therefore
proceeded to the work, Daniel's opinion to the
contrary notwithstanding.

Henry first drove down a stake by the bunch
of Kalmia, to which he fastened his line, then

measuring forty feet on the brook westward, it reached the Azalea, where he drove down another stake, and drawing his line tight made it fast to that also; then measuring forty feet to the north at right angles as near as possible, he drove down the third stake and fastened the line as before. Then before any further progress was made, he squared this angle, which he did in this way. First measuring eight feet from the corner of the angle to the east, and driving down a stake; then measuring six feet from the corner to the north and driving down another; then laying his ten feet pole across from one of these stakes to the other, he found it did not reach, which proved it was not square; he was therefore obliged to take up the stake and line at the north and bring it in, until it touched the ten feet pole, and then drove it down again.

Having one corner square, there was no difficulty in finding the place for the stake for the remaining corner.

And now to get the centre of the square, a line was stretched from corner to corner diagonally, and near the centre a mark with a stick made beside the line ; then removing the line to the other corners, stretched it again, and where the line crossed the mark that had been made a stake was driven down, that being the centre.

Having thus found the centre, he proceeded to strike out the circular beds and alleys. — Beginning at the stake in the centre, he measured three feet towards the outside of the square and put down a stake : this was for the arbor, and in this circle he put down the birch poles ; then measuring two feet more, which made the outer edge of the inner circle; then one and a half feet for an alley ; then four feet for the outer edge of the second circular bed ; one and a half feet for another alley ; then four feet more for the third circular bed, and lastly three feet for the wide alley; and at the end of all these measures a stake was put down.

Having fastened the line loosely upon the central stake, he commenced striking out the circles; at the first stake, three feet from the centre, he tied into his line a sharp pointed stick; holding the stick perpendicular, in his hand, and keeping the line tight, this first circle was described on the ground. He proceeded in the same way with the others until all were completed.

With much delight Margaret saw the outlines of the plan upon the ground, and having expressed her approbation of her brother's skill, returned to the house by her flower beds, where the Crocuses were in full bloom, opening their petals of brilliant hues to the bright morning sun, and the Snow Drops so gracefully and modestly hanging their heads among the foliage. Some of the Narcissuses were beginning to show their flower buds — and the progress which the Tulips, Crown Imperials, and Hyacinths had made, plainly told that a thousand new beauties were about to unfold themselves.

Daniel having now returned, was directed to take a spade and throw the soil from the part marked out for the alleys on to the beds. Great care was observed not to get over the marks. Henry next laid out the alley from the outside of the square to the arbor, two and a half feet wide. — The beds were now raked fine, the circles again described, and the narrow strips of turf laid evenly round, and settled into the ground with the back of the spade, the edges trimmed, and the soil thrown upon the beds, and again raked.

The next thing that Daniel did, was to wheel from the brook gravel for the alleys, which was rather a heavy job. — They were filled nearly as high as the turf, and made perfectly level.

In the meantime Henry made the arbor, which he did by first setting down birch poles each side of the walk on the inner circle, then taking a stick two feet long, and measuring round the circle, he found there was room for seven more, according to the plan, which were put down that distance apart.

Care had been taken to select such poles as were straight and of the same size. The tops, which had been left on, were brought over and woven or tied together.

Henry now had the pleasure of seeing the plan completed, and although wearied with the toil of the day, stopped some time and viewed with much satisfaction the work of his hands.

Margaret joined him, and was highly gratified with the appearance of the garden. — Their attention was now arrested by the robin, which had cheered them in the morning, and who had taken his stand upon the elm, and was chanting his evening song in thrilling notes.

Henry. We listen with peculiar pleasure to his sweet and simple song, as it is associated with the opening season, verdant fields, and fragrant flowers.

Margaret. Where do you suppose the robin has been through all the cold winter?

H. After they have reared several broods of young, and their food begins to fail, they begin to emigrate to the south, very leisurely, stopping wherever good living is to be obtained. Indeed they are so tardy, that they are often overtaken by snow, which quickens their flight. A few stragglers are to be found in warm sheltered places throughout the country in winter : but the general rendezvous is in the most southern states, where they perch at night in the thick cane brakes, and there become an easy prey to those who are disposed to kill them, which can be done with a stick.

Their progress to the north again, is with the

opening spring; and this straggler comes now, as it were with the welcome prelude to the general concert about to burst upon us from all the green woods and blooming orchards.

M. The robins seem to be more social in their nature than most of the feathered songsters, building their nests, and rearing their young, even in our gardens; don't you remember the nest of robins in ours last year?

H. Yes; and I have no doubt, but this one on the elm is one of the same family, and means to confide in us for protection as he did last year.

M. Well, I think he will be very safe so far as we can defend him; you know that some boys are so unprincipled as to shoot them; I am sorry there are such; it proves they are thoughtless and destitute of fine feelings, and if all indulged themselves in such a cruel practice, our fields and orchards would be dreary and sad, compared to what they now are.

H. Not only should we be deprived of their animating songs, but worms and other insects would so increase, that the labors of the husbandman and gardener would almost be in vain, and the foliage of the trees would be so disfigured by the caterpillar, canker worm and other greedy insects, as to present a sad and melancholy aspect.

M. I should not think the little birds could make so much difference in that respect.

H. You would be astonished to know how many caterpillars and other insects are consumed by a single pair of sparrows and their young in one day.

M. Do you suppose any person ever knew ?

H. Yes, very nearly ; I recollect of reading once of a person, who took his seat near the nest of a sparrow, and watched them all day, and kept an account of all that were consumed.

The old ones were busy picking young

caterpillars from a neighboring tree, and conveying them to their young, who greedily devoured an astonishing number. — It is some time since I read the account, and I cannot say positively, but think the number consumed was something like 300 for the whole family, which would make more than 2,000 in a week.*

M. I should not think it possible.

H. I was so impressed with the important assistance they render, that I never from that time threw a stone at one of the useful creatures, as some are wickedly and wantonly in the habit of doing.

M. I suppose that birds generally are not so useful as the sparrow and robin ; for in talking with our school-mate, James, the other day for his wanton destruction of birds, he excused himself by saying he did not kill any but such as did damage.

---

* See Note at the end of the work.

4

H.   I think he ought to include himself in
that list; for they only take a little from his
father's field, and repay for that little by their
destruction of insects; while he gets his whole
living and makes no return, but to lounge
about with his gun, with Jowler at his heels, to
destroy what God has wisely given for our
pleasure and interest.

M.   James is not so much to blame as his
father, who is to be pitied; and although he
has enough of the good things of this world, is
destitute of the finer feelings, and rather laugh-
ed at our father, for spending so much time in
the garden with dear mamma and ourselves,
and keeping us all the time at his heels, as he
expressed it, when papa had been telling him
of the advantages of a kitchen and flower garden, as a place of discipline, instruction and
amusement for his children. — You know they
are destitute of a garden, and James has nothing to do when out of school but hunt and fish.

And as for fruit, you know they have nothing but crab apples which are fit only for cider.

H. You mistake, dear sister, they have a notable garden.

M. Indeed, I never saw it ; do describe it.

H. I was sent over one day of an errand, and while I was there it was discovered that the hogs were in the garden ; which you know we should consider a great calamity.

M. Oh, dreadful.

H. James and I were sent to drive them out, and in so doing I had a chance to see it for the first time. — The garden was situated directly back of the pig-stye, in the centre of a patch of something like half an acre of potatoes of most luxuriant growth, whose tangled tops were finely intermingled with aspiring pigweeds, and Roman Wormwood, occasionally garnished with a huge Sunflower full ten feet high, and flowers a foot in diameter, standing like sentinels to watch their precious charge. It was about three rods square. In one corner I saw a clump of Marigolds, Four o'Clock, Prince's Feather, and a few other common annuals, huddled together, striving to live, as well as their neighbors, the pigweeds. In a bed there was a small quantity of beets, carrots, &c., that looked as if they were quite forgotten. A portion was occupied by a few hills of corn and beans ; and cucumbers, squashes and melons were so thickly located in the remainder, that I wondered how it was possible to gather the fruit, if there should happen to be any, without destroying the vines.

M. You give a sad account of it. I hope we shall be able to keep ours in better taste.

H. I expressed my surprise to James, at the appearance of the garden — who replied, that his father had not much taste for a garden and thought it was foolish to spend as much time as some of his neighbors did in it : but I have wandered from the subject of birds. I know of but few birds, although they may be troublesome at times, but are upon the whole a great benefit ; and a person is without excuse who wantonly destroys them.

M. We are staying out late ; let us go to the house. Do notice, how merrily the frogs sing ; they appear to partake of the general happiness, with which all animated nature seems to be filled. Where do you suppose they live in the winter ?

H. They bury themselves in the mud at the bottom of the water and remain in a torpid state — as do also the turtles and toads.

M. Now the garden is ready — when shall you begin to sow seeds ?

H. If the weather is pleasant, I will sow some of the most hardy tomorrow. I conclude

you have finished your plan for the disposition
of the perennials, in fanciful groups as I pro-
posed.

M. Yes, I have. Shall you move the bulbous roots this spring?

H. No. That cannot be done without
injury or total destruction at this season of the
year, and wherever they have been introduced
in your plan, must be omitted until the proper
season of planting, which is the autumn.

The next day, Henry commenced the sowing of the most hardy annuals, such as are
marked with a star in the catalogue.

With a stick two and a half feet long, the
beds were spaced off one foot from the edge,
and the number sticks put down, as laid out in
the plan. Then round the stick of such as
were to be sown, a circle was made one and a
half feet in diameter, in which the seeds were
sown. He had received some general instruc-

tions for sowing seeds from a friend, which were these : — For very fine seeds, the earth should be sprinkled very lightly and finely on, and not covered more than a quarter of an inch deep, and pressed down hard with a trowel or something of the kind. Larger seeds covered in proportion to their size ; and those as large as a pea, to the depth of an inch or more. Very delicate seeds will require some protection from the mid-day sun, as it is apt to burn them up when they first appear,— and the ground must be kept moderately moist, if the weather should be dry. Damp meadow moss will do very well to lay over the plants in the middle of the day. Great care must be taken to keep the young plants free from weeds.

Some may think it a difficult thing to distinguish so many different kinds of plants from the weeds, when they first make their appearance. The way Henry did, was first to become acquainted with the weeds which infested the garden ; and then, when examining his beds for the appearance of plants, he knew at once what might be pulled up with safety.

The seed being sown in circles round the stick, he knew exactly where to look, to find the plants, and if any appeared in or near the circle that was new to him, naturally concluded that it was the plant sown.

I shall not now describe the different groups of perennials, but will do it as they come into bloom. The work of transplanting them was all done in the course of the month ; the early flowering kinds in the first part of it.

The roses and other shrubs were all moved as soon as possible, and planted on the outside of the square. The tops of the rose bushes should be cut off, which causes them to bloom stronger. Perennial and biennial seeds should be sown in a bed by themselves, and moved to the flower garden, when of a proper size. As a general rule, the seeds should be rolled into the ground with a roller, or pressed in with a board, as some kinds will not otherwise vegetate ; and even then will be destroyed by exposure to a scorching sun, unless attended to every day, until they have established themselves.

A child may not know the meaning of annuals, perennials, or biennials.

Annuals are such as are sown in the spring, flower, ripen seed, and die in the fall, as the Marigold, Four o'Clock, Cucumber, &c.

Biennials are sown one year, and flower the next, produce seed and die, as the Canterbury Bell, Beet and Carrot.

Perennials are sown one year, and flower the next in most cases ; but sometimes not until the third, or even fourth year. After this, they continue to flower year after year.

Such as die down to the ground every fall, and spring from the root next season, are called herbaceous, as the Columbine, Sweet William, Asparagus, &c. Those that do not die to the ground, and form woody stems, are called woody, as the Rose, Currant, and Lilac.

Roots are of different kinds, as the branching, fibrous, bulbous, tuberous, and spindle. Branching roots are like the branches of trees, as the roots of all trees. Fibrous roots are composed of thread-like fibres, as the roots of all grasses, Sweet William, &c. Tuberous are fleshy, like the Potato, Pæony, Dahlia. Bulbous roots are of different kinds ; as solid, like the Turnip and Crocus ; coated, like the Onion and Hyacinth ; and scaly, like the Lily ; spindle, like the Carrot.

Indigenous plants are such as are natives of our own land. Exotics are those introduced from foreign countries.

The perennials for the first part of April were red and yellow Crown Imperial, different varieties of the Crocus, Snow Drop, Persian Iris, Heart's Ease, exotics ; and Liverwort and Blood Root, indigenous ; and for the latter part of the month, Hyacinth of different kinds, Narcissus, Venus's Navel Wort and Corydalis, exotic ; and Wild Anemone, and Violets, from the woods.   About the middle of the month, Henry and his sister were in the garden, before school, sowing the seeds with this mark, †. There had been much unpleasant weather the past fortnight, cold storms of rain and even snow, — but they found that some of the seeds that had been sown had begun to vegetate.   It was necessary to rake the ground a little before sowing, as it had become hard on the surface by the frequent rains.   While thus engaged, they were startled by an immense flock of red winged black-birds, sweeping suddenly over their heads, with a noise like a tempest, which after a few circuitous, whirling flights, showing their black dress, ornamented by the vermilion red of their wings to the best advantage, settled upon a large red maple below the garden in the meadow. The tree itself, an object of admiration, at this season of the year, covered with its showy scarlet flowers, was beheld with silent astonishment as its branches literally bent with its noisy visitors clothed in their funereal plumage, contrasting elegantly with the flowers of the tree. They commenced such a concert of discord and harmony, that it might be heard for more than a mile; each performer appearing to exert himself to be heard above the rest. After continuing their clamorous concert for a few minutes, as if by common consent, they suddenly commenced their social, chattering flight to a distant part of the meadow.

Margaret now broke silence, which had only been interrupted by exclamations of wonder and surprise, and observed that the blackbird was one that James had proscribed, as worthy of death, whenever he could get a good shot.

Henry. They are, to be sure, troublesome to the farmer in autumn, when their flocks, increased by their offspring, almost darken the air by their numbers, as they drive like a furious tempest over the tempting cornfield. Yet it is not generally considered or perhaps known, that the injury, however great it may be, is much more than overbalanced, by the immense number of insects and their larvæ which they destroy as their principal food, and which are of the most injurious kinds to the farmer.

It is remarked by Kalm, a Swedish traveller in this country, and whose name Linnæus gave to the beautiful Kalmia that adorns our garden, that in 1749, a bounty of three pence per dozen was offered for these birds, by government, which caused a great destruction among them. The consequence was, that the Northern States experienced a complete loss of the grass and grain crops, which were now destroyed by insects.

Margaret. It seems to me then that the farmer, who would destroy these birds because they take only what is their lawful wages for the sake of adding a little more to his store, is like the covetous dog in the fable — who when crossing the brook with a piece of meat in his mouth, and thinking that his shadow was another dog with a piece of meat, caught at it, and in so doing lost what he had. — Will you tell me where these birds reside in the winter?

Henry. Early in November they leave the Northern States, with the exception of a few who linger on the sea coast or the Middle

States, for the more southern part of the Union, where they stay until the return of spring; and then wing their way to the north, relieving the fatigue of their long passage by their friendly gossip. They reach this part of the country from the first of March to the middle of April, according to the season.

M. Do see how these plants of Heart's Ease flourish; it is but a few days since you moved them, what a variety there is already.

H. I was careful in moving them, and the early flowering perennials, as well as the biennials, to take up a large portion of earth with them that the bloom might not be checked. Such as are more tardy, can be moved with more certainty of success, even if they are divided or cut to pieces, if necessary to increase the kind. But as a general thing the roots should not be much disturbed, to insure a strong bloom, when moved in the spring.

M. Look, I have gathered twelve varieties of the Heart's Ease, or Lady's Delight for mother, and also some flowers of the Navel Wort; what a neat little azure blue flower it is, — what is its botanical name ?

H. It is called Omphaloides verna, and is very common in the cottage gardens in England and would be here, if more generally known. Here are some flowers of the Corydalis to add to your nosegay, with its singular shaped, pendulous pink flowers. This will be in bloom a number of months.

M. The Violets and Liverwort are beginning to show their pretty flowers. They are the emblems of humility, and overlooked because they are to be seen in every pasture and wood, but I like them none the less on that account.

H. We will take up some more, when it will not interfere with our studies. Do notice the flowers of the Blood Root, what a lively, brilliant white. It has a fleshy tuberous root, which, upon being wounded, discharges a blood colored fluid, with which the Indians stain themselves.

M. Here is the Wild Anemone, which is so fond of the shade; I fear it will not succeed well here. It does not make much show, but its solitary, bell shaped flower, white, and externally red or purplish, looks very modest, as it rises from its low three leaved stem.

H. Now we have looked at our plants here, we will take a look at our bulbous roots before school.

M. As we go, will you get me a branch of the willow on the brook, which I see is in bloom.

H. Here it is; but in getting it I disturbed a company of the song sparrow, or as it is generally called, the ground bird.

5

M. Is it the same that sings so sweetly in the morning ?

H. It is, and arrives about the time of the blue bird.

M. Is the chirping bird a sparrow ?

H. Yes. But he is a different species from the song sparrow, who is rather more retiring than the chirp bird, and builds his nest on the ground. The chirping sparrow builds his nest on low trees, in the orchard, or by some frequented walk, on a shrub. You know there has been a nest of them in our front yard every year, either in the Lilac or Rose bush, and last year they took possession of the Honeysuckle that runs up the pillars of the piazza. His song is very indifferent, being only a complaining chirp. There are several other kinds of sparrows, described by Mr Nuttall in his book of Ornithology, which you will find a very interesting work.

M. I should like to read the book very well.
See how grand our Crown Imperials look ; they
are at least a yard high : how rapidly they have
grown ; where is its native place ?

H. It is a native of Persia. I will show
you the nectary of the flower, as it is called ; it
is quite a curiosity. You will observe at the
bottom of each petal a leaf, a white glandu-
lar cavity, with a drop of limpid juice standing
in it.

M. O, I see, they look like pearls. The
flowers hang their heads in such a way, that a
person would not notice this beauty unless they
paid particular attention, or raised the bells a
little ; how gracefully the luxuriant stem, adorned with broad shining green leaves, is crowned
with its whorl of pendulous flowers.

H. There is another wonder about this
plant ; the flower stems, that now hang down,
after the leaves or petals fall, turn and become

upright, as the seed ripens. Here we have the yellow and red, — but there are many more varieties cultivated ; among the handsomest, is the gold and silver striped leaved.

M. The Crocuses are beginning already to fade. I think they are a great ornament to the garden, as they come into flower as soon as the snow is off.

H. It is said to be a native of Switzerland, and the flower in a wild state is white with a purple base, — and by cultivation all the numerous varieties have been obtained. The Hyacinths are beginning to show their colors. — Here is a Persian Iris.

M. How sweet it smells — and what a delicate blue, with violet spots. The flower has no leaves.

H. The flowers first make their appearance and afterwards the leaves. The Narcissus, as well as everything else, is in rapid progress.

There is the curious Hoop Petticoat Narcissus;
the long nectary, I suppose, gives it the
name. Take it, for we must go to school.

MAY

MAY DAY.

Henry. Today is a holiday and we have liberty to take a walk, and collect wild flowers, or amuse ourselves in the garden, as we please.

Margaret. There is such a heavy dew, we cannot go until the grass is dry, so let us go into the garden and see how it flourishes.

H. Have you noticed the swallows and martins?

M. Yes, I saw the martins yesterday, they came to the boxes : the blue birds had taken possession and claimed them. A battle followed ; the martins were strongest, and drove off the intruders.

H. The martin is a beautiful bird, and seems happy to place himself under the protection of man. Secure in his asylum for himself and family, he twitters out his gratitude, and is everywhere received with welcome. — When they appear we may venture to sow our half hardy annuals. But we will first look at our Hyacinths and Narcissuses, which are now in perfection.

M. O, they do look sweetly; here is one that wants tying up, the bells are so heavy that it lies on the ground; it is a delicate pink.

H. That the Dutch call Groot Voorst, which means my good wife; that dark purple with the petals tipped with green, is called Indian Crown. The name of the splendid single red is Henrietta, and the pure white one, Pyrenne.

M. There is one light, and another dark blue, and another that is straw color, and others that are white with red and purple eyes. What a wonderful variety; here are twelve Hyacinths, and no two of them are alike.

H. There is indeed a variety to us; but to a florist, who has seen hundreds of varieties in the highest perfection, our collection would appear rather indifferent.

M. Is it possible that there are so many varieties?

H. I have read that more than a thousand varieties are cultivated in Holland, as an article of commerce at the present time, with each a name. When the rage for Hyacinths was at its height, about a hundred years ago, there was double that number under cultivation, differing in some small degree from each other, and some of them highly prized. As much as ten thousand dollars has been known to be given for a single root, and much more than that has been offered and refused. Since that time the taste for this and other bulbous roots has declined, and at this time the highest price in the Dutch catalogue is sixty guilders or about twentyfive dollars. The common price for a mixture of good sorts is from twentyfive cents to one dollar a root, and multitudes of the poorer sorts are annually sold at auction for a trifle.

M. I am astonished at your account of the Hyacinth, its numerous varieties, and value. It does not seem possible to me, that any person could be so foolish as to give such an enormous price for a single root, beautiful and fragrant as it is. How long has this superb flower been cultivated?

H. It is not certainly known; but it is supposed to have been introduced by the Dutch in the beginning of the sixteenth century, soon after the revival of commerce in the west of Europe, when the merchants of Holland traded to the eastern shores of the Mediterranean, and the Archipelago. It is a native of the East, and is abundant about Aleppo and Bagdad, and is blue in its wild state.

M. The Narcissus cannot be compared with the Hyacinth. Yet I think the Incomparable very fine; the little bright yellow petals, so handsomely disposed between the large white ones, make a handsome contrast, and I suppose give it the common name of butter and eggs. The smell is not disagreeable to me, although some dislike it.

H. It is said that the smell has a dangerous effect upon the nerves. The name is from a Greek word signifying *stupor*. For this reason the Narcissus was consecrated to the furies, who by means of it, were said to stupify those whom they wished to punish.

M. Then I am sure I will smell of it no more, for I have no desire to come under their influence, and I want all my senses to enjoy this fine day.

H. The early Tulip looks lively, but much inferior to the stately late ones, which now only show their green buds. We will go and sow our seeds, and make some observations in our new garden, and then, if this east wind does not cheat us out of our pleasant day, (for I perceive it has this moment changed into that quarter,) we will see what we can find to amuse us in the fields and woods.

The seeds sown today are those in the catalogue with this mark, ‡. *(See pages 22—27.)*

The perennials in bloom, were Violets of different kinds, among which, the double sweet scented arrested their attention, before they reached the spot; the flowers of this sort are used by chemists to detect an acid or an alkali.

The Dwarf Phlox, the pink and the white, were beginning to show their lively flowers,

and also the Dwarf Iris. The flowers designed for the first part of this month, were the Golden Alyssum, Early Tulip, Narcissus and Jon-
quille. The Scarlet Columbine, including the
numerous golden varieties, Honesty, Daisy leaved Catchfly, and Solomon's Seal, with the noble
Late Tulip and White sweet scented Narcissus,
for the latter part of the month. They had
also a fine root of Periwinkle in bloom. Margaret was admiring the beauty of the flowers and
foliage, when she was startled by a toad, the
first she had seen. She said, O, Henry, here is
your old friend, the toad; I don't know how it
is, but I never can be reconciled to his ugly
looks; and still you were so kind, as to make a
shelter for him from the sun last year.

Henry. Although he is not a beauty, I
think he is not to be despised; he does his
part in exterminating the enemies of the gardener, and as he is fond of a cool place, sheltered

from the scorching noon day sun, I was pleased to lay boards upon stones, or bricks, that he might have a comfortable retreat.

M. I know a man, who offered the boys in his neighborhood, a certain price per hundred, for all the toads they would bring, to put in his garden; but it is an article, I think, I should not like to deal in.

H. I have been reading, in White's Natural History of Selborne, of some ladies, who took a fancy to a toad, which they nourished, summer after summer, for many years, until he grew to a monstrous size.

M. They must have had a singular taste.

H. The reptile used to come forth every evening from a hole under the garden steps; and was taken up, after supper, on the table to be fed. But at last a tame raven espying him, as he put forth his head, gave him such a severe stroke with his horny beak, as to put out one eye. After this accident, the creature languished for some time and died.

M. It is the last creature I should think of taming. Brother, do you perceive how cold it grows? I must retire to the house, and shall be glad to shut myself. up in a warm room, rather than take the walk.

H. There is a wonderful change in the weather, which is not very uncommon, in this changeable month; for some of the most delightful days terminate the most uncomfortably. I perceive we shall be compelled to find our pleasures, the remainder of the day, in the house, in conversation and books, rather than in the fields as we contemplated. I will take the opportunity to look over your plants in the sitting-room, as some of them want attending to.

Having returned to the house, and while Margaret was engaged with her book, Henry

was busy looking over the pots of flowers.—
Among them was a pot of Chinese Primroses,
with which he was so much
pleased, that he thought he
would make a drawing of
it. After an hour's close
application, he presented
the work to his sister, who
was much pleased with it,
and wished him to give a
history of the plant.

PRIMULA SINENSIS.

Henry said, that the botanical name *Primula*
was derived from the word *primus*, the first
to flower. The delicate blossoms of many of
the species appear in their native regions,
when all nature is otherwise inert. The
genus includes a great variety of beautiful
dwarf alpine plants, among which are the Eng-
lish Primrose, Cowslip, Polyanthus and Au-
ricula ; some of which will stand our winters,

if placed the north side of a fence or wall, but are more liable to be destroyed by our powerful summer sun. The Chinese Primrose is more delicate, and is, strictly speaking, a green house or parlor plant. It was introduced from China in 1820, and is now a popular ornament to both the green house and parlor. This one is pure white, another variety is purple.

Henry went out and looked at the thermometer, and was astonished to find, that the mercury had fallen from 70 to 35 degrees, in the course of three hours. A cold storm followed, which prevented them from attending much to the garden. Pleasant days succeeded, and all their leisure hours were spent in admiring the thousand opening beauties before them. Among other objects that attracted their attention, was the American Cowslip, which lined the margin of the meandering brook, as far as the eye could see, giving a brilliant yellow shade to the bright green verdure of the meadow. Large masses of the Rodora, beginning to unfold their rich purple flowers in fine contrast with the Cowslip, ornamented the banks of the brook.

Some new bird with ever varying note, was to be seen, or some flower bursting into life and beauty, on each returning day. By the tenth of the month, the leaves of the oak " were as big as a squirrel's ear," which according to the Indian proverb is the proper time to plant corn. Henry took the hint, and planted the remainder of his tender annuals. A few Dahlias, which he had given him, were planted at this time, in the quarter marked S. He found too, that the weeds began to prevail, and as he considered that the beauty of a garden consisted much in neatness, and remembering James' garden, he set himself to work in earnest in their extermination.

The 15th was a lovely day, over which Flora seemed to preside, and as there was no school, it was agreed, they would take a ramble.

In passing through the orchard, which was in full bloom, and whose fragrance filled the air, they observed the bees swarming over the trees collecting their honeyed sweets, and other insects of all descriptions revelling in the profusion before them. Suddenly the golden robin with his fiery plumage, appeared to their view, full of life and activity ; now darting into concealment among the rich clusters of flowers, then again appearing, uttering his lively note. How lovely, exclaimed Margaret ; what can he be so busy about ?

Henry. If you will but pay particular attention, you will see that he is feeding upon the insects we have noticed ; his nimble movements are necessary, or his active prey will evade his vigilance. See, he seems occasionally to take a sip with the bees, by way of variety.

Margaret. How much there is this morning to amuse us, and lead our minds up to Him, who has filled the earth with his goodness, and who has for our gratification, given us the varied and fragrant flower, the beautiful bird with his gay plumage and exhilarating notes, and all the pleasant scenery before us.

H. But there are thousands who have eyes to see, and ears to hear, and yet pass the beauties of creation unnoticed, and see not God in his lovely works, and instead of going on their way rejoicing, are filled with misery and complaint, and go mourning and grumbling to their graves. Our dear father says, this is in a great measure owing to a deficiency of early education; their minds not having been directed when young, to admire the works of the Most High.

M. I never shall forget the instruction our father gave me when I could hardly speak. I was with him in the garden, admiring a bed of splendid Tulips; their gaudy colors attracted my attention, and I wondered who it was that could have given them their rich shades. I innocently said, " Father, who painted the Tulips?" He said, " My dear, it is God;" and then went on to tell how he had made all things. His conversation so raised my curiosity, that I was incessantly asking him questions about the great God.

H. Let us never despise those who cannot see the beauties we see. For while we have had kind and tender parents, who took the advantage of every incident and every thing to enlighten and amuse us, — they have been neglected by parents, who perhaps, had their perceptions blunted by the too free use of the polluting and degrading bottle.

M. Now men are coming to their sober
senses, and looking with disgust upon the in-
toxicating cup, and discountenancing those
who use, or traffic in the abominable thing,
may we not hope the next generation will be
more enlightened and happy?

H. There is no doubt of it...... Here is
a Geranium.

M. A Geranium?

H. Yes; it is the only indigenous species
that has any claims to beauty. It is commonly called Crane's Bill; the petals are pale
purple. Now we will keep along by the side
of the hedge in the open field.

M. The men are busy in planting. Hark!
I hear a cat in the bushes.

H. You are mistaken, it is a bird; do you
see it hopping from bush to bush? how shy he
looks, and into what queer attitudes he suddenly throws himself, constantly upon the
move.

M. His plumage is a dark slate color.

H. It is the Cat bird; when alarmed, he makes that curious noise, something like the mewing of the cat.

M. It is a singular cry; but he has changed his note. He can sing, if he has a mind; his notes are now pleasant, but the poor bird sings as though he was almost choked with grief.

H. Their songs are said to be variable, some being much finer singers than others.....

M. O, these rocks are covered with the Scarlet Columbine, growing from the clefts and crevices.

H. And in company with them is the Saxafrage, with its white, sweet scented flowers.

M. Hark, brother! do you hear the song of that bird? it exceeds anything we have heard. He makes the thickets ring with his melodious and varied notes.

H. Let us set down on the rocks and listen ; it is the Red Thrasher, by some called the Planting bird, but his proper name is the Thrush ; he seems to give grateful utterance of praise to the beneficent Bene'actor, for the profusion and beauty by which he is surrounded.

M. Now his song ceases, and there he goes ; how he spreads his full tail as he flies.

H. There goes his mate after him, their plumage is a kind of cinnamon color. See, they have settled upon that large oak. Hush, he has commenced his song again.

M. How touching his notes, — how cheering it must be to the farmers in the field yonder, who are so busily planting...... Casting their eye toward the woods, near by, they observed the edges of it highly ornamented with small trees completely covered with flowers of a pure white ; — they immediately directed their steps to them, and found it was the Shad Blossom or Wild Pear. An abundance of the Choke Cherry was also in bloom, with its racemes of white and yellow flowers.

Having gathered some of each, they struck into the thick and luxuriant wood, by a winding pathway, and admired the various shades of the tender leaves. The Peewink, or ground Robin, was to be seen, hopping under the thick under brush, diligently seeking his food, uttering forth his monotonous notes; while the lofty trees were vocal with a multitude of birds unknown to them. They stopped to admire, and gather some of the flowers of the Cornus Florida, which were gracefully intermingled with the foliage of a thick Hemlock. Henry was obliged to climb the tree, as they were out of reach. Soon they came into the meadow, which was alive with the Bob-o-link and other birds. Henry told his sister what Mr Nuttall says, in his Ornithology, that the boys of this part of New England, make him spout among other things, the following ludicrous dunning phrase, as he rises and hovers on the wing near his mate : " *Bob-o-link, Bob-o-link, Tom Denny, Tom Denny,—Come pay me the two and sixpence you've owed more than a year and a half ago ! — 'tshe, 'tshe, 'tshe, 'tsh, 'tsh, 'tshe,* modestly diving at the same instant down into the grass as if to avoid altercation."

Margaret observed, as one flew immediately over their heads, that he did seem to say so, and thought that it was not wonderful that he should feel ashamed of himself, after such an impudent dun, and hide in the grass. Their walk was continued on a causeway over the meadow. As they passed the bridge over the brook, they disturbed a Peewee, who was building a nest under it, and whose well known pleasant notes, had been heard amid the agreeable jargon of innumerable bob-o-links and black birds, that seemed to revel in the broad green meadows.

As they reached the hill, they found the ground carpeted with Violets, and the Dwarf Ranunculus, with its brilliant yellow flowers, and under the shade of the handsome flowering Thorn and other shrubs, the Bell Wort and Wild Anemone flourished.

Arrived at the top of the hill, they sat down under the shade of a beautiful clump of trees, from whence there was a fine view of the surrounding country, which seemed like a blooming paradise.

While viewing the delightful scenery, they discovered a Fish Hawk sailing majestically over the meadow below, in wide circles, moving with such apparent ease, that it seemed as though it was done without any exertion of his long curving wing. Suddenly he stopped his course, and for an instant flapped his wings, and then rapidly descended for his prey, in the brook below. As he arose, the little birds which seemed to have been much alarmed at the presence of the intruder, encouraged by the bold King bird, commenced, with loud cries, a general attack upon him. Tormented by the King bird, who flying above him, sorely harassed him, he made a precipitate retreat, followed by all the noisy inhabitants of the meadow, who seemed to triumph in his defeat, until he was fairly escorted to his own woody premises.

Having indulged themselves in beholding the beautiful landscape below, they returned home by another route, richly laden with the flowers of May.

About the 20th, the Tulips were in perfection, and as they were admiring their beauty, Margaret requested her brother to give a history of it.

Henry. The Tulip is a native of the Levant, and has been in cultivation nearly three hundred years, and may be called the king of florists' flowers, as no flower can claim equality with it, in the brilliancy of its endless combinations of all colors and shades.

It appears to have been brought to Europe from Persia, by way of Constantinople, in 1559; and in a century afterwards, to have become an object of considerable trade in the Netherlands, and a sort of mania among the growers, who bought and sold *single bulbs*, at prices amounting to three thousand dollars each, and upwards ; in those days an immense sum. The taste for Tulips in England was at its greatest height about the end of the seventeenth and beginning of the eighteenth century. It afterwards declined, and gave way to a taste for rare plants from foreign countries.

The Tulip, however, is still extensively cultivated in Holland, from which all Europe and America is still supplied with bulbs, and also to a considerable extent in England.

The varieties of the Tulip are endless. — There are a great many of the double sorts, which are fine, also of the Parrot Tulips, which have notched petals and striped or diversified with green, and also of the early flowering varieties ; but the most grand of all are the late flowering varieties, which are without end. As many as a thousand varieties are cultivated with names.

Margaret. It is no wonder it was called a mania, for those who paid such prices must have been mad.

H. It degenerated into a mere gambling business, and was rightly named " Tulipomania." The Tulip is supposed by some to be " the lily of the field," referred to in Christ's Sermon on the mount.

The whip-poor-will was first heard this evening and listened to with pleasure.

Henry. I have heard it said by some superstitious persons, that whatever we wished when we first heard the whip-poor-will, would come to pass — but I think it very foolish and wicked, to pay attention to such nonsensical notions.

M. It will do no hurt to wish that we may become better.

H. Nor any good, unless we *strive to become so*, as well as *wish*.

Many shrubs were now in flower, as the Lilac which had begun to fade, the Snow Ball, and the herbaceous plants mentioned for the last of May*; and by the last of the month others not enumerated had begun to show their flowers. Particular attention was paid to keep the garden free from weeds — and to stir the earth round the perennials.

* See pages 22—27.

JUNE.

Margaret. This is the month for Roses and many other beautiful plants.

Henry. Here is a fine Cinnamon Rose; it is very fragrant and fresh with the morning dew.

M. Thank you, brother. It is but a week since I picked the first opening bud, and now I perceive the bush is full of them.

H. It is the earliest hardy rose we have, and is the forerunner of a superb family, which not only please the eye with their beauty, but regale us with their unrivalled fragrance.

M. If the Tulip is *king*, I will crown the

7

Rose, the *queen* of flowers.   The Rose, I believe is common to all countries.

H.   Yes, and is known to every body at first sight, and has been a favorite flower from time immemorial among all civilized nations.

M.   Are there as many varieties of the Rose as of the Tulip or Hyacinth ?

H.   Yes ; the shrub varies in size from one foot to six or eight, in different species — and the colors are red,   white,   yellow,   purple, black, striped ; simple, or in almost numberless shades and mixtures ; and single, semi-double, and double.   There is also a great variation in the leaves and stems, — some are climbers, covering hundreds of yards : so that there are an immense number of varieties under cultivation, exceeding the number of either Hyacinths or Tulips.

M.   Where have all these varieties been obtained ?

H. A great part of them have been raised from seed within the last forty years, in Europe and in this country.

The Scotch and the Damask will next come in bloom; and will be quickly followed by the Blush, White, York and Lancaster, and Provence; and our native Roses last of all.

The perennials for the June quarter, were the following. Spotted Stalked Phlox, with purplish red flowers; Sweet scented Phlox, with pure white flowers; Iris, Pæony, Blue and White Spiderwort, Sweet William of different sorts, Fox Glove, Snapdragon, Monk's Hood, Dame's Violet, exotic; and Perennial Lupin, and Bird's Foot Violet, indigenous.

Particular care was necessary to keep down the weeds, during the whole of the month.

The annuals were thinned out, and such as were wanted, to mix with the perennials, were transplanted the last part of the month

with a scoop trowel, taking a plenty of earth
with the roots. The plants in the second
inner circle, were supplied with brush.

The surface of the ground was kept light
and no weeds suffered to appear.

The little garden looked very neat, and was
the admiration of all who saw it. Henry's
taste and industry were highly commended.—
Some of the annuals began to expand at the
close of the month, among which was the
Azure Blue Gilia, —with its delicate flower,
in heads, and finely divided leaves ; the
Scorzonera very showy in the morning, and
which continues in bloom till autumn, — with
orange yellow flowers and purple centre, and
dandelion shaped leaves ; and the Catchfly, a
popular flower, very showy.

Summer now seemed to have gained the
ascendency. The foliage of the leaves was of
the deepest and most brilliant green, and seem-

ed to invite to their cooling shade. Henry
made a rude seat under the wide spreading
elm, which was a favorite retreat to himself
and sister ; and here, secure from the burning
sun, and fanned with the gentle breeze, many
pleasant hours were spent in reading and in
examining flowers; while above their heads in
the thick luxuriant branches, numberless yellow
birds made the air vocal with their pleasing
notes. The Golden Robin, too, claimed a
part of the tree as his domain, for on its long
swinging branches, he had built his nest, and
seemed busy in his domestic concerns ; while
the swift Swallow, as though he was afraid
there would be a lack of amusement, was
circling round the tree, almost with the rapidity of lightning, nimbly feeding upon his active
prey.

Here they were seated on a warm June day,
with a great variety of fresh gathered flowers.

As Margaret was admiring the Monk's Hood, she observed that she had heard it pronounced a poisonous plant.

Henry. It is a deadly poison, and should be known to all who cultivate it. Linnæus says, that an ignorant surgeon prescribed the leaves, and on the patient refusing to take them, he took them himself, and died.

Some persons, only taking the effluvia of the herb in full flower into the nostrils, have been seized with swooning fits, and have lost their sight for two or three days.

Margaret. The whole plant is curious and handsome ; but the terrible account you give of it, seems to balance the beauty, and I shall look at it for the future with suspicion.

H. Here is the Digitalis or Fox Glove, which, though very beautiful, is a violent poison ; but is valuable in medicine. There is no danger of being injured by handling these plants.   No one should put any kind of plant into his mouth without knowing its properties. Little childre n should not be suffered to run in a garden without attendance ; for I have heard of one who lost his life, by eating the flowers of the Columbine.

M.   Is it possible ! how careful, then, should we be.   Here is the Phlox ; it is one of the most showy plants we have, and I like it much, because some of the species are in flower the whole season.

H.   The Sweet William, however common, is a beautiful flower ; and one of the most con- spicuous ornaments of this month and the beginning of next.

M.   The variety with bright purple flowers with white border, I think as pretty as any.

H.   I found that upon a heap of rubbish, I had thrown out of the garden, -and suppose there were among it some stalks of the Sweet William, in which was seed.   It is curious to observe, how many varieties will be produced from the same plant.

M. The Spiderwort has very rich flowers, but it is to be regretted that it is so soon destroyed by the sun.

H. But to make up that deficiency, it continues in bloom all summer, and adds much to the interest of a morning's visit to the garden.

M. Why is the Fleur de Lis called the Iris ?

H. From its great combination of colors; which with its unique appearance, has ever found admirers, among the curious and scientific. There are a great many species and varieties; we have only the dwarf and common garden sorts.

M. Is not the Blue Flag we see in the meadows, an Iris ?

H. It is, and looks very gay with its blue flowers, with the Golden Senecio and a multitude of other flowers, that now add richness to the waving grass.

M. Can anything equal the splendor of this Pæony?

H. No class of flowers has attracted more attention of late, than this in Europe and America. Many superb varieties have been introduced from China, which throw this, beautiful as it is, quite in the back ground. The species you hold in your hand, was introduced into Antwerp a little more than two hundred years ago, and then sold for an enormous price.

M. It is common now in every garden, and justly considered worthy of the highest place. Nothing can exceed the richness of its crimson petals, and if other kinds are superior to this, I should like to have them.

H. There are as many as fifty different species and varieties; some a pure white, blush, and shades of red and purple; but the price of them is so high, that we must content ourselves without them.

M. How curiously the Snapdragon springs open, when the thumb and finger presses the sides of the flower.

H. It has the appearance of some creature's mouth, which, I conclude, gives it the name.

M. What is the reason the Perennial Lupin has succeeded no better in our garden?

H. It is almost impossible to transplant it with any success. The only sure way to have it in perfection, is to sow the seed where it is to remain. I have some growing from seed, and shall have this beautiful indigenous flower in abundance next year.

M. We saw large beds of it the other day, along the edge of the sandy shrub oak wood, which were very showy.

H. There is a singular circumstance in the manner in which the seed is scattered for propagation. When the pods become perfectly dry, they suddenly open with a spring, so as to throw the seeds to a great distance.

M. The many different ways in which seed is dispersed, are truly wonderful, and cannot fail to give exalted views of the wisdom of the Most High.

H. The Bird's Foot Violet is a companion of the Lupin, and is so named, on account of the leaves resembling a bird's foot. They have flourished finely in our garden, and would look very pretty for a border to a bed.

M. The Hesperis, or Dame's Violet, scents the whole garden with its highly odoriferous flowers.

H. There is a double kind, which can be propagated only by parting the root, and which is highly prized.

They were much amused now by some Humming birds. A pair of them was seen busily engaged, rapidly darting from flower to flower, collecting their delicious fare. Presently another one appeared, and began to collect his share of the sweets ; but others thinking they had the best right, darted upon him, and quicker than thought, their shrill cry was heard high in the air.

Having driven the trespasser far away, the jealous birds returned, and seated themselves on a dead limb of a bush near by, much to the gratification of the children. Soon the intruder returned, but with no better success, for the pair seemed to have taken possession, and claimed the spot as their own.

Henry thinking they must have a nest near, commenced a search, and after a close examination of a neighboring apple tree, found the puny and well concealed nest, upon one of its branches. So much did it appear like the moss which covered the limbs, that they were delighted with the ingenuity of the little bird.

Henry had the curiosity to climb the tree, and look at the nest, which was exceedingly neat, with eggs the size of peas ; but perceiving the agitation of the little bird, who darted within a few inches of his head, he made a hasty retreat, not willing to disturb so lovely a creature.

At the close of the month the Kalmia Bush was in bloom. Some of the woods near by were profusely ornamented with this most beautiful indigenous shrub. The Azalea was in bloom the beginning of the month — of which there were two species ; one with red flowers, in dry woods, the other in low grounds, with white flowers, both ornamental and fragrant.

Honeysuckles now displayed their beauties, gracefully winding up the pillars of the cottage, perfuming the whole house with their exquisite fragrance.

As soon as the foliage of the Tulips began to turn purple, the roots were taken up, and laid in a shady place to dry — as also the Crocuses; the Crown Imperials too were moved the last of the month.

Hyacinths are longer in coming to maturity. In about two months from the time of flowering, when the leaves begin to turn yellow, which is about the middle of July, they should be taken up and treated in the same manner as the Tulips.

JULY.

LATER sorts of Roses are still in bloom, but much infested with the ravenous rose bug.

Many troublesome insects now begin to swarm. The Pinks and Lilies, with the following perennials, were found in bloom in the July quarter, in the course of the month, viz: Perennial Larkspurs, Double Feverfew, Coreopsis, Scarlet Lychnis, Spiræas, Phloxes, Mullein Pink, and Canterbury Bells, a biennial.

Many annuals in the course of the month showed their flowers, among which were the Convolvulus Minor, Candytuft, Chrysanthemum, Coreopsis, Dwarf Rocket Larkspur,

8

Scarlet Cacalia, Evening Primrose, Balsams, Beautiful Clarkea, and Yellow Hawkweed.— The arbor too began to be covered. As Henry had labored with unwearied diligence the past month to keep down the weeds, very little difficulty was now experienced, as the plants had obtained a good growth.

The plants were tied to neat sticks as they advanced in height, to prevent them from being beaten down by heavy rains or high winds. All flower stalks were cut off after flowering, except such as were wanted for seed, and all with straggling branches neatly trimmed.

One Carnation root graced the garden, whose opening flowers were the peculiar care of Margaret. She tied up its long stem to a piece of green wire, stuck into the ground.— One superb flower had expanded. The ground of it was white, elegantly variegated with scarlet and deep purple, and full three

inches in diameter.   She thought it surpassed
all the flowers that had been in bloom, wheth-
er they had charmed the eye by their beauty,
or regaled the sense of smelling by their fragrance.   As Henry came to her, she said she
hoped he would save all the seed, as such a
rich flower should be more plenty.

Henry.   The flower is double, and of course
there will not be any seed.   New varieties are
raised from semi-double sorts, grown in the
neighborhood of fine double ones ; and then,
perhaps, out of five hundred seedling plants,
one may be as handsome as ours.

Margaret.   How then are the fine double
kinds multiplied ?

M.   By what is called *laying*. After the
plant is done flowering, or before by some, the
sprouts you see at the bottom of the plant, are
laid in the following manner.   An incision is
made a quarter of an inch below the second or

third joint from the plant, and the knife passed
up to the centre of the joint. It is then peg-
ged down with a hooked stick, and buried half
an inch deep. In a short time they throw out
roots, and may then be taken up and put in
pots, or planted out in a bed. They must be
well protected, or they will very likely be injured by the severity of the winter.

Double Pinks can be propagated in the same
way ; or by dividing the roots when they have
done flowering.

They can be increased by piping, which is
nothing more than cutting off the sprouts entirely, and setting them in small pots, which,
if covered with a tumbler, will form roots.

The Carnation was unknown to the an-
cients, but has been cultivated in Europe time
out of mind. Very little is known of it in its
wild state, although it has been found on the
south side of the Alps, and very rarely in

England. The botanical name, *Dianthos*, is from Greek words signifying, *the flower of God*, or *divine flower*, on account of its pre-eminent beauty.

Margaret. The fine Double Pinks are not equal to the Carnation, but still they are superb; and you say they are more desirable, because they are so hardy. We have two varieties, the one with rich purple centre and white border, so finely fringed, is my favorite: it is two and a half inches in diameter.

H. I don't agree with you: I think the other is the handsomest; the centre is deep crimson, bordered with fine blush — almost destitute of any fringe, — and the flower is as large as yours.

M. The common kinds do very well when none of the superior sorts can be obtained, as they have the same exquisite fragrance; but one fine variety is worth fifty of them.

H. An immense number of varieties of Carnations and Pinks are cultivated by florists.

M. Do you observe the White Lily perfumes the whole garden?

H. The Lily is considered the emblem of purity. We have two species indigenous. The Canada Lily, with yellow spotted drooping flowers, may be seen the last of June, or the first of this month, in wet meadows. The Philadelphia Lily, now in bloom in dry pastures, with red erect flowers, is the other species. We have also in the garden, the Orange Lily, with upright flowers; and a great many other beautiful species are in cultivation in some gardens.

M. Don't you think the Larkspur a showy class of plants?

H. I do; which do you consider the handsomest?

M. Of the annuals, the Double Dwarf

Rocket is by far the prettiest. See what a variety : — there are rose, white, lilac, blue, purple, and variegated ; and then the flowers are so full and thick, they form very dense spikes.

H. The Double Branching Larkspur is fine, with the same variety of colors ; but the flowers are not so large or thick. Of all the species that I am acquainted with, the Double Perennial is the most grand ; this we find in bloom from June to October, displaying its azure blue flowers in such long rich spikes, full three feet high, that they fill every beholder with admiration.

M. I should say the Dwarf was the prettiest, the Double Perennial the grandest, and and the Bee the most curious. The Perennial Bee Larkspur before us is at least four feet high, erect, and crowded with blue flowers, the central part having the exact appearance of a bee.

H. The Perennial Grand Flowering, with its large, various colored brilliant flowers, is also very showy, and continues a long time in bloom. Here is a double kind I raised from seed : the flowers are a cerulean blue, variegated with purple ; and upon the whole, taking the class together, they are very interesting, and very desirable, on account of their easy culture, great variety, and beauty.

M. What curious little flower is this ?

H. It is the Beautiful Clarkea, called by botanists, *Clarkea pulchella;* it is exceedingly neat and handsome. It was discovered by Capt. Clark, at the mouth of Columbia River, and named after him.

C. PULCHELLA.

M. Was it the same who accompanied Lewis on the exploring expedition to the Rocky Mountains ?

H. It was ; had it not been for them and other adventurous travellers, we never should have been in possession of such a variety of beautiful flowers.

M. Here is the Coreopsis ; was not this brought from the West.

H. Yes ; we are indebted to Mr Nuttall for this, who found it on the prairies near the Rocky Mountains, and as it seeds very freely and is perfectly hardy, it is now found in most gardens. It is not only ornamental, but continues long in bloom.

Some varieties of the Perennial Coreopsis are very beautiful ; the Broad Leaved I think most choice.

M. My favorite, the Variegated Euphorbia, I believe was introduced by Nuttall from the West, and in my opinion it is one of the handsomest plants in the garden in September.— The beauty of its variegated green and white leaves is unrivalled.

H. The American Centaurea, a singular thistle like flower without prickles, was discovered by him on the banks of the Red River, and comes in bloom next month. . . . .

M. I can now pick a bouquet of flowers exceedingly beautiful.

H. Let me see a specimen of your taste.

M. The Double White Spiræa, or Queen of the Meadow, of snowy whiteness — Double Scarlet Lychnis, rich blue — Azure Blue Gilia, light blue — Coreopis, deep yellow, with rich brown centre — Yellow Hawkweed, pale yellow with purple centre — Purple Candytuft, fine purple — Lobel's Catchfly, pale red — Divaricate Phlox, purplish red — Mullein Pink, Common Pink, and Ten Weeks Stock, deep red — Lavender, light green — Hyssop, dark green.

Henry. Very good : you might have added,

of the Double Feverfew, called by botanists, *Pyrethrum parthenium*, which is very pretty ; its white flowers are a great ornament to the garden. It is an exceedingly neat border perennial, about two feet high, producing a great abundance of white flow-

P. PARTHENIUM.

ers, and continues in bloom a long time. It is a native of England, and generally cultivated and greatly admired in the cottage flower gardens in that country. — It should be sown on finely pulverized soil, lightly covered, and rolled down hard, or it will not vegetate. — When young, transplant it into borders where it is to remain.

The two first you named, are the most superb perennials, and can be propagated only by dividing the roots.

M. The Convolvulus Minor is beginning to open its rich tricolored flowers.

H. It opens about seven or eight o'clock, and continues from one to four in the afternoon, depending upon the heat of the sun. — We shall have it in perfection for three months to come.

M. The sun begins to be uncomfortably warm, and I must go to the house. I will take one of the Wild Roses and add to my nosegay, and present it to mother. . . .

H. How busy the hay-makers are in yonder meadow; I am going to spread swarths for them.

M. I admire to hear the sound of the whetting scythe, and smell the fragrance of the new made hay. Goldsmith says he pities the person whose taste is so perverted as to prefer the smell of musk, civet, &c. to the delicious fragrance of new mown hay, the Sweet Briar, the Honeysuckle, and the Rose ; and whose ears are ravished by the squeaking fiddle, but will be offended by the notes of the

Thrush, the Blackbird, and the Nightingale.
I almost wish it was the fashion for girls to
lend their assistance in haying, as in old times.

Henry took hold of the fork in good earnest,
and worked very diligently, though he was
somewhat disturbed by the bees, who seemed
to have settled thickly about the meadows;
and though he had been taught not to hurt any
creature, he could not forbear fighting them,
especially after he had been severely stung
once or twice.

After having slightly refreshed themselves,
Farmer Thrifty, who did not mean to rust out,
observed that they must make hay while the
sun shone, and leading the way, was cheer-
fully followed by his hale and hearty fellows,
whose good constitutions had not been poison-
ed by rum, and commenced the work of turning and raking.

The heat now seemed insupportable; not a

breath of air was stirring; the birds lately so
noisy were silent in the shade; and all was still,
save the chirping of the grasshopper and crick-
et, or the singing of the locust, and the occa-
sional ominous note of the tree toad on the tree
above. No clouds intercepted the powerful
noon-day sun; only a few white fleecy ones
were seen slowly moving in the far distant
west.

As they lay reposing after dinner on their
outer garments, a low distant sound of thunder was heard. The farmer was immediately
on his feet, and, looking anxiously to the west,
directed their attention to a white cloud at a
great distance, towering like a mighty moun-
tain, with its summit clothed with eternal
snow; another distant peal brought all his
workmen upon their feet, and without any
urging they were quickly and nimbly at work,
and soon the hay that was ready for the barn

was loaded into the carts, which were handy in the field. Every nerve seemed to be strained as they beheld the cloud, rising and blackening, and assuming every moment some new and fantastic shape, as they heard the frequent thunder nearer and nearer ; and now another cloud was seen swiftly rising in the north, and thunder answered to thunder as the hollow sound reverberated from one quarter to the other ; and as the clouds darkened, the frequent lightnings seemed to play with greater brilliancy as they darted from cloud to cloud. By this time the hastily loaded teams were hurried to the barn ; the well fed and managed oxen partaking of the spirit of the times, swiftly, and with apparent ease drew their ample loads to a place of safety. And now, without the loss of a single moment, the men commenced raking what remained. . . . . They were not a little amused with their neighbors the other side of the brook. A black jug and a paper of brown sugar had been seen in their possession. There was such a whipping and shouting to the unmanageable, and apparently deaf cattle as almost to drown the noise of the approaching tempest, which now enveloped the distant hills with a whitish mist, and was seen waving the trees of the nearer forests. At this critical moment an unlucky wight drove directly into a slough, and there the load stuck fast,* and was left to the fury of the tempest, which now came furiously over their heads. Farmer Thrifty had just finished the raking of his hay, when the big drops began to fall ; but before the men could reach their outer garments the rain came down in torrents, accompanied with such vivid lightning as almost to take away the sight, instantaneously followed by tremendous peals of thunder. Some were for flying

* See page 104.

to the tree for shelter, but they were told of the danger, and that the open field was the most secure place ; and soon they were convinced of this, for immediately there came a flash of lightning that seemed to envelope the whole meadow with fire, accompanied by such a deafening clap of thunder, as almost to stun the amazed spectators, and fill them with astonishment as they saw the tree rent, and its limbs scattered over the ground. They now with rapid speed, made their way to the house, carefully avoiding the trees, whose prostrate branches showed the fury of the tempest.

Henry reached the house, as wet as if he had been in the brook ; but soon had his wet clothes exchanged for dry ones. The shower now seemed to have spent its fury : the thunder appeared less heavy, and at a greater distance — some seconds intervening between the flash of lightning and the report ; the rain

9

quite abated, and the hoarse thunder was heard rolling in the distant east, and the lightning seen beautifully playing among the black clouds; when suddenly, the sun broke forth and looked upon the scene, which produced a full and perfect rainbow. The children were enraptured with the sight, and could hardly express their joy, as they noticed the bright green foliage of the distant trees, contrasted with the black eastern clouds, surmounted by the noble arch, with all its brilliant colors, faintly repeated so as to appear double; — soon it gradually vanished away.

Henry found that the tempest had done damage to the garden; prostrating and breaking plants, and washing away the soil. But in a few hours the following morning, all was set to rights again. The grass edging was trimmed with a large pair of shears, so that it looked as neat as ever. This operation had been performed once before.

White Water Lilies were found in abundance in a neighboring pond, which was often visited for this universal favorite, which so enlivens the ponds of New England.

AUGUST.

THE continued warm weather is favorable for insects, which now seem to revel in every shape, from the most beautiful butterfly to the humble worm; noisy with mirth, unconscious of the cold frost, that is soon to sweep them from existence.

Among the most prominent is what is commonly called the August bird, whose dull monotonous note, at the close of the day, seems to tell of days misspent and privileges abused, and friendly warns us of the rapidity of time, and of approaching eternity, and the importance of improving the remainder of our days to the best advantage.

Early in the month, our young friends were highly amused, in observing the red and yellow butterflies, whirling round in playful company; now lighting upon the margin of the still brook — then flitting from flower to flower of the milkweed, and other showy plants that lined the margin of the stream; while the larger and more gaudy species were to be seen in their more solitary flight, mixing occasionally with the puny tribes. The Dragon Flies, with long needle-like body, and transparent wings, mingled in the sport, as they rapidly skimmed over the surface of the smooth water. In the evening twilight might be seen moths of every description. One species in particular arrested their attention, (as they were looking at the Evening Primroses,) which was hovering about this flower and the Four o'Clock. Henry supposed it was a species of Humming Bird, until he caught one, and found it was a large, beautiful Moth. He was greatly astonished when his father told him it was produced from the nauseous green tobacco worms. . . . . As the darkness increased, the Fire Flies enlivened the meadows with their numerous brilliant lights, — the air resounded with the noise of myriads of insects ; and to give variety to the scene, the large Bull Frog would occasionally be heard in deep guttural bass. The Toad, too, as he sat half immersed in water, was not a whit behind his neighbor, in point of musical talent, as he occasionally joined the chorus in shrill and lengthened notes.

The following group of flowers was to be seen in the quarter for August.*

In the rear was the stately perennial double flowering Sun Flower, with its beautiful dahlia-like flowers; with the magnificent red, and the red and white Hibiscus, and the Dou-

* See pages 22 — 27.

ble China Hollyhock, red, black, yellow and white: — before them, the superb Cardinal Flower, with incomparable scarlet flowers — the white and purple Pyramidal Phlox, whose stalks it was necessary to support, on account of the load of its flowers — the Purple Rudbeckia, the Tiger Lily, with stems tall and erect, with numerous glossy leaves, each ornamented by a black berry-like bulb, terminating in a chandelier top of numerous black spotted, orange flowers — the Dwarf Solidago, with fine yellow — the Fulgent Rudbeckia, with yellow and brown — the Coxcomb, deep crimson, and the Prince's Feather, with deep red flowers. The Yellow Swallow Wort, too, ornamented this group with rich orange flowers, — a native of sandy fields.

Nearly all the annuals were this month in bloom, and the arbor was completely covered with a profusion of foliage and flowers; so that the whole circle of plants made a most gorgeous show, which could only be appreciated by those who saw it. Very little was to be done but the saving of seeds, cutting down decayed plants, and tying up and trimming; so that now, all their toils seemed to be more than repaid in all the beauty and variety before them. With seats in the arbor, it was a delightful retreat during the hours allowed for recreation.

The Thunbergia Alata, or Winged Thunbergia, was now to be seen every morning with its yellow and purple flowers; this plant was first cultivated in England, in 1825, and has proved a great acquisition to our flower

THUNBERGIA ALATA.

gardens. It is a climbing perennial, easily raised from seeds, and comes into flower the first season, when quite young, and continues to produce numerous beautiful yellow flowers, with a rich purple centre, for many months. — It grows well in pots in the parlor, with a small trellis, and will endure a slight frost without injury.

As they were viewing the Mimosa or Sensitive Plant, one fine morning, Margaret remembered and repeated Dr Darwin's beautiful and expressive lines upon it.

> " Weak with nice sense the chaste Mimosa stands,
> From each rude touch withdraws her tender hands ;
> Oft as light clouds o'erpass the summer glade,
> Alarmed she trembles at the moving shade,
> And feels alive through all her tender form,
> The whisper'd murmurs of the gathering storm,
> Shuts her sweet eyelids to approaching night,
> And hails with fresher charms the rising light."

Henry. His description is just and beautiful. The sensibility of the plant is worthy of particular attention and admiration.

Margaret. How has this sensibility been accounted for ?

H. Dr Darwin says, naturalists never have explained the immediate cause.

M. At the approach of night, how curiously the leaves meet and close together, as though asleep.

H. And not only at night, but at all hours of the day, the least touch, or concussion of air produces the same effect ; and if the leaf stems are touched, as though hung with hinges on the main stem, they instantly drop; presently recovering and resuming their former position; so that a person would be induced to think they were really endowed with the sense of feeling.

M. I have noticed when it was very hot, the plant was most irritable — and when quite cold, very slightly so.

H. Every change of weather seems to affect it ; so that it may justly be esteemed one of the most wonderful plants. It is said that a curious Calabrian philosopher, upon observing the nature of the plant, without being able to discover the cause of its sensibility, became insane. We may learn something from this plant.

It would be foolish for us to say there was no such thing as a sensitive plant, (now plainly before our eyes,) because enlightened men cannot explain the cause of its sensitiveness. But would it be equal to the folly of saying there was no God? or that we did not believe that he existed from eternity? or in the other doctrines of the Bible relating to himself, which are as plainly revealed to us there, — as this plant is to our eyes — because they cannot be comprehended by enlightened reason! It is no wonder men become insane, like the Calabrian philosopher, when they attempt to explain or to look into things too high for the human mind.

M. May we never be left to doubt, because we cannot understand the mysterious doctrines of the Bible.......

H. The Ice Plant, I think a curious and splendid plant, on account of the ice-like crystals which adorn and cover the succulent leaves and stems.

M. I hope you have one of these, and the Sensitive Plant in pots, as the first frost will destroy all in the ground.

H. I have not only these, but other tender annuals potted..... The Yellow Escholtzia *(Escholtzia californica,)* is a beautiful plant, and was first grown in England in 1826, from seeds transmitted from California. Each plant forms a wide patch of decumbent stems, covered with a fine,

E. CALIFORNICA.

healthy, glaucous foliage, upon which repose

hundreds of rich yellow flowers, unfolding their interior, of a dazzling brightness, under the influence of the sun, but closing at the approach of rain. It is a perfectly hardy plant, thrives best in an open, dry, light soil, and flowers from June till destroyed by frost. It should be sown early, in a frame with a little heat, and turned into the open garden after it has acquired ten or twelve leaves.

What a profusion of morning flowers now adorn the garden; the arbor, with the numerous varieties of the Convolvulus, and different varieties of the Flowering Bean, agreeably intermingled, make a splendid show.

M. But of all the creepers, the Cypress Vine, with its abundant deep green feathery foliage, and crimson flowers, may be considered first; this, with the deep orange of the Nasturtium, and the various colored fragrant Sweet Pea, and curious Balloon Vine, matted together, give the inner circle a gay appearance. (See page 19)

H. Among the many beautiful morning flowers, I think the Commelina is not exceeded by many.

M. Nothing can surpass the brilliancy of the fine blue of its three-leaved flower, with the same number of rich yellow stamens ; but they are soon destroyed by the hot sun ; the stems and leaves look a little like grass.

H. I shall take up the roots in October, and keep them in the cellar with our Dahlias, as the roots, like them, are tuberous.

M. The African Hibiscus, and Bladder Ketmia are also beautiful morning flowers, but soon perish.

H. The African Hibiscus *(Hibiscus vesicarius)* is much superior to the other varieties, being much larger, and is the size of a common teacup ; the petals are a

H. VESICARIUS.

delicate straw color, with rich purple centre, adorned with a cone of numerous golden stamens. To make amends for its frailty, it is very hardy, and continues to send forth a long succession of flowers.

M. The fragrant Balsams are to be seen at all times of the day. It seems to me I have never seen so handsome ones as ours; the flowers are as full as Roses; some are variegated, others crimson, scarlet, purple, white and pink — not a single flower among the whole.

H. I have been careful to pull up every single and semi-double one, as not worthy of a place in the garden. The double varieties produce seed sparingly. I shall save every seed, as it improves by age, and will be good ten years hence.

M. A multitude of other plants show their flowers from morning to night, as the Chrysanthemums, Zinnias, Marigolds, Amaranthus

Lavateras, and many others that so profusely decorate the garden; among others, the **Tangiers** Scorzonera (the *Scorzonera tingitanum* of botanists) is a very hardy annual, and is very showy, particularly in the morning—being covered with bright yellow flowers a long time through the season. Why don't you have some of the beautiful Gerardia, that is

s. TINGITANUM.

now so ornamental to the woods, and looks so much like yellow Foxglove?

H. I have taken up the roots repeatedly, but with no success, and my efforts this year to raise it from seed, have also failed.

M. There are two species, I believe.

H. The oak leaved is the handsomest; the flowers are variegated with brown, but soon perish. Most of our perennials now in bloom, are inhabitants of some part of North

10

America, and in point of beauty may well compare with any exotic.

M.   The Cardinal Flower, I think, cannot be surpassed in the richness of its scarlet.

H.   Our brook has an abundance on its banks, and although fond of water, it seems to flourish here with greater luxuriance.   These plants I raised from seed, but they succeed very well if taken up before or after flowering; if part of the garden is wet, that is the best place for them.   In point of richness of color, the Dwarf Solidago and Orange Swallow-wort, both abundant in our dry pastures, may be classed with the Cardinal Flower.   The Swallow-wort has long thick roots like a parsnip, which may be dug even when in bloom, as ours was, and set out in the garden, and will flower well the next year.

M.   I have not seen the Hibiscus wild, nor the Phlox.

H. I have not; but they are found in some parts of the country.

M. Here is the Grand Flowering Argemone; you say it is from Mexico; it looks somewhat like a large white Poppy, but is more delicate, and very ornamental, as it is always in bloom. . . . . The Crepis Barbata, or Purple Eyed Crepis is uncommonly beautiful and hardy, and of the easiest culture. It should be sown in masses, and thinned out to eighteen inches' distance. It continues to flower from the first of July to October,

CREPIS BARBATA.

during which time it is covered with beautiful blossoms, the petals of a light yellow, finely contrasted with a brilliant purple centre. It grows wild in the south of France. . . . .

By the middle of the month they were highly amused by the swallows as they congregated on the roof of the barn, as if in deep consultation about their contemplated journey; occasionally taking a circling flight, then settling down again eagerly engaged, as if some important question was under discussion; and as night approached, they seemed to adjourn to the brook, and might there be seen, settling upon and bending the bushes almost to the water by their numbers — resuming again their business at the usual place early the next morning.

Among the evening flowers that attracted their attention, was the Marvel of Peru, or Four o'Clock, of different colors, and which continues with the morning flowers, until, like them, destroyed by the sun; this opens about four o'clock. Another species, the Long Flowered, with white flowers and purple centre, standing on long tubes, and fragrant, is very firm, but perishes before morning.

They were pleased oftentimes to go after sunset, to watch the opening of the Evening Primroses, which are the grand evening flowers.

Margaret. The Mignonette emits a delicious fragrance, as the dews of the evening begin to fall.

H. It is very desirable on that account, and continues long in bloom, and is one of the plants I should not like to have absent, though the flowers have but little claim to beauty. Now watch this Grand Flowering Primrose. You see the four green leaves by which the flower is enclosed, and which is called the calyx; they are hooked together at the top, and enclose the flower, which you observe is anxious to expand, by the parting of the calyx below, and showing its yellow petals.

M. Now it seems to be at a stand.

H. It is acquiring force to unhook the calyx at the top, which seems to be disposed to keep it under control, as in times past, when in infancy and youth.

M. There! then it burst the calyx and is free, but it is not fully expanded.

H. It has exhausted itself in the struggle; it waits a moment to recruit; now it has spread out quite flat.

M. How curious it is to see them popping out so thick; they give a sickening perfume to the garden.

H. Here is the Long Flowering, standing on long tubes; this, with the other kind, keeps company with the morning flowers a while; but here is the elegant low spreading species, with pure white flowers, which loses its beauty before morning; all that is then to be seen, is the shrivelled flower, changed to a pink color.

M. The Night Flowering, I think, is also a beautiful species; its habits, like the last, are delicate, and the blossoms are found perished in the morning.

SEPTEMBER.

ALL the annuals come into flower this month which have not bloomed before. The most showy is the large family of China Asters, Sweet Alyssum, Variegated Euphorbia, Scarlet Malope, Purple and Yellow Immortal Flower, Purple and White Amaranthus, Cockscomb, and a multitude of others.

The perennials are the splendid Dahlias, which are now in perfection, the New England Star Flower and Solidagos, with their numerous species and varieties, which also profusely adorn the meadow, wood, and fields; and many other perennials continue in bloom, which have been noticed.

Little is to be done in the garden but to pick up all decayed leaves and plants, and to transplant and divide perennials, which should be done by the first of this month, or the last of August, or sooner.

The nights now begin to grow cool, and fears are often anticipated, that a frost will destroy the beauty of the garden, now in the height of grandeur, which fears are often realized by the last of the month, and sometimes before, and do partial injury.

The Dahlia is the grand object of admiration this month; and although it produces flowers frequently through the summer, they are not equal to what are seen now.

Margaret. Our Dahlias are superb; you were so careful to put down stakes, and tie them up and trim them, that they make a majestic appearance; there is at least a dozen of the purple, now in full bloom, and nearly as

many of the scarlet, with many buds in pro-
gression; what a pity it is that they must so
soon be destroyed by frost; what can be
richer than the colors? and then the plant is
so tall and grand, that I must say, as I have
before of other flowers, that this is the finest.
I should admire to see a large collection of
them, of all colors and shades, as I have heard
there were numerous varieties cultivated. Do
tell me something about its history.

Henry. It was named after a Swedish
botanist, by the name of Dahl, a pupil of Linnæus. It is also called Georgina.

It is but a few years since it was known in
this country, and was but little cultivated in
England until 1814. It is a native of Mexico,
and the first introduced into Europe was a
purple one, in 1789, which was single.

Double ones of three colors were first
known in 1802; since then the varieties have

been astonishingly increased; and now such varieties as a few years ago were considered beautiful, are thrown away to give place to the more splendid sorts which are annually produced from seed.

M. Will they flower the first year from seed?

H. Yes; but most of the flowers will be single; perhaps one in a hundred, or more, will be a fine double one, if the seed is of a good quality.

M. How then are the fine varieties propagated?

H. By dividing the roots, which are tuberous, and resemble the sweet potato very much; as soon as the frost has blackened the tops, they should be dug up and put into a warm and dry cellar, secure from frost. When spring returns, they must be divided by a sharp knife, being careful to leave a bud on each tube, or else they will not grow. Gardeners also raise them by cuttings.

M. I hope we shall be able to obtain some new varieties in the spring.

H. The China Asters make a good show now; we have some of the finest, which are the Double Quilled of different sorts, and variegated.

M. The Immortal Flowers, with the Amaranthus, are desirable on account of their permanency; I shall cut the greater part of them to ornament the mantel-piece in the winter.

H. They look very well when no fresh flowers are at hand; I have understood they will retain their color for years.

M. I shall cut some of the elegant Cockscombs, too, before the frosts.

H. The Euphorbia can be preserved so as to retain in a great measure its beauty, by being dried between paper, and pressed.

M. That will be fine ; with that, and the Purple, White, and Yellow Immortal Flower, the Purple and White Amaranthus, and Red and Yellow Cockscomb, I can make quite a gay bouquet for winter.

H. The Scarlet Malope is a beautiful ornament to the garden, on account of its coming in and continuing so late, as well as the beauty of its althea shaped flower.

M. The Sweet Alyssum is another that I like on that account, with its numerous little fragrant white flowers.

The principal perennials not before mentioned in the September quarter, were the New England Star Flower, or native Aster; many of these species combined presented a fine show ; here were as many as a dozen different sorts, with various shades of purple, blue, rose and white, and laden with a profusion of different sized flowers ; some fine species of the

Solidago were mixed in with them, all of which Henry selected from the fields the last year when in bloom, and transferred them to the garden. A late species of the Phlox, with its red flowers, gave life to the whole. A few of the annuals now in perfection were mingled in with them; some fine Altheas, also in bloom, on the back side, added beauty to the group.

The garden continued its gorgeous appearance until the last of the month, when there came a frost sufficiently heavy to destroy the tender annuals, which, when the sun arose, gave them a blackened and melancholy appearance; these Henry soon removed, and the garden was not entirely destitute of beauty, for many plants remained as bright as ever. The Dahlias were partially injured, but warm weather following, they seemed to revive and flower as well as ever.

OCTOBER.

A FEW slight frosts appeared to have affected the trees in a singular manner. The large Maples in the meadow had changed to a deep red ; the foliage of some trees was of a bright yellow ; others were turning purple — every shade from green to yellow, and from yellow to red and purple, might be seen in the surrounding forests.

The first half of the month was remarkably pleasant ; Margaret thought it the most delightful part of the year, while she rambled about the woods with Henry gathering nuts.

The leaves were beginning to fall from the trees, which reminded them of the approach of winter, yet there was much about the forest that gave them pleasure. The squirrels were engaged in the same employment as themselves, laying up a store of nuts for the winter, from the profusion scattered over the ground.

The striped squirrel attracted their attention, as he was seen nimbly gliding to his store-house, occasionally stopping to reconnoitre the intruders, his cheeks swelling with the load.

The red squirrel made the woods resound with his whirring, secure on the top of some tall pine.

A grey squirrel was seen running on a prostrate tree; suddenly stopping, and quietly seating himself with tail erect, he began to indulge himself with a chesnut, which he conveniently held to his mouth with his fore feet, quickly hopping on a tree, as the children made a movement to get a nearer view.

Margaret. What singular bird is that descending from the tree before us ?

Henry. It is not a bird, but the curious flying squirrel ; see! another flies ; they have landed at the foot of that dead tree ; now they run up the tree and enter a hole.

M. It is strange that a squirrel should fly. Have they wings like birds ?

H. They have not proper wings, but a skinny substance, covered with fur, in the same manner as the body, which extends from the hind to the fore feet. They cannot, like birds, rise in the air, or even horizontally, but descend from the tops of trees obliquely, as we saw. . . . . . . Now we have filled our baskets, we will return ?

M. Hark ! is that thunder ?

H. No ; it is the drumming of the partridge.

M. How do they contrive to make such a noise ?

M. It is done by the male bird, as he stands in the midst of his family, on a prostrate log, parading with erected tail and ruff, and drooping wings — very much like the turkey. Suddenly he commences flapping his sides with his wings, with increased rapidity of motion, which produces the tremulous noise we have just heard.

As they passed on through the woods, they started up a flock of Partridges; the sudden noise occasioned by their flight at first alarmed Margaret, until Henry told her what they were.

They were gratified with the sight of a Rabbit in the path before them, who for an instant timidly watched them, and then glided into the bushes.

The beautiful Blue Jay was frequently seen flying from tree to tree, uttering his noisy notes. The crows were seen in sable dress, in

11

lengthened lines, in their sluggish, silent flight, as they passed over the meadows to a distant wood.

An abundance of Wild Asters and Solidagos continued to ornament the edge of the forest, and on the banks of the brook, the Black Alder showed its brilliant scarlet berries; the Clematis made a fine appearance, as it stretched its long trailing branches from bush to bush, covered with bunches of seeds, with their curling, feathery tails.

Margaret picked a bunch of the Barrel Flowered Gentian on the margin of the brook, which she thought were buds, which its deep blue flowers resemble, until Henry told her they would not expand any more.

But the most elegant flower of this month is the Fringed Gentian, which they found in abundance in the meadow. They very much admired its delicate, bell-shaped, blue flowers, with fringed border.

Some of the most hardy annuals mentioned last month, continued still to display their flowers. The most conspicuous were the Scarlet Flowered Malope, which seemed to flourish in spite of frost, — Sweet Alyssum, with fragrant white flowers — Immortal Flower of various sorts; Dahlias continued until the middle of the month; Gentians, Solidagos and Asters, indigenous plants, and some other perennials, showed to advantage in the October quarter.

The Early Blush Chrysanthemum was much admired, and also some beautiful varieties in pots, which Henry had nursed with care, and which now began to ornament the sitting-room.

Margaret. There is nothing that equals the beauty of the Chrysanthemum at this season; how does it happen that the flowers are so much finer than they were last year?

Henry. It is owing to different management. Last year they were put into large pots, when they were taken out of the cellar in the spring, with common garden soil, and no attention paid to trimming, but grew up with numerous stems; the pots being crowded, produced but few and small flowers.

This year I was more particular. I had prepared in the fall a compost of two thirds well rotted turf, and one third decayed scrapings from the cow yard, which were well mixed together and left in a heap until wanted for use. In April I took some small sized pots, and filled them with this compost; in each pot I put a single sprout, with a small piece of the root of the old plant. They were then set in the window, and by the last of May had grown half a foot or more; they were then shifted to a pot one size larger, and plunged into the ground in a shady place; if any suckers appeared at the bottom, they were taken off. In the course of the summer, the operation of shifting was performed twice more; the last time, in August, into large sized pots. I was careful to tie up the stems to a neat stick as they advanced in height, and watered them occasionally with liquid manure. Before any frost appeared they were put under shelter.

M. Those buds that have opened are twice as large as they were last year; the plants are so tall and healthy, one would hardly believe they were from the same stock.

H. The Chrysanthemum is a universal favorite with florists, and is very ornamental to the green house and parlor, when but few other plants are in bloom.

The Chinese are very fond of this flower, and from them all the beautiful varieties, amounting to as many as fifty or sixty, have originated.

The first was brought into England in 1764; latterly most of the varieties have been introduced.

Henry planted the remainder of the bulbous roots this month ; the Lilies, Crown Imperials, and Pæonies having been planted in August. Holes were dug one foot and a half deep, and filled with a previously prepared compost of one third fine river sand, one third decayed scrapings of the cow yard, and one third well rotted pasture turf.

Polyanthus, Narcissus, Pæonies, Crown Imperials, and Lilies, were planted five inches deep from the top of the bulb ; Hyacinths, four inches ; Tulips, Narcissus, and Jonquilles, three inches ; and Crocuses and Snow Drops, two inches.

NOVEMBER.

HARD frosts the beginning of this month destroyed nearly all the flowers. From what remained, Margaret picked a bouquet, in which were the Scarlet Flowered Malope, Sweet Alyssum, Scarlet Monthly Honeysuckle, Bee Larkspur, China Pink, Immortal Flower, and Heart's Ease.

The Dahlia stalks having been cut off near the ground, the roots were carefully dug, and laid on a shelf in a warm dry cellar. Some roots of the Commelina were also taken up and put with them.

All the flower stalks were cut off, and at the close of the month, the perennials were covered with pine boughs, to secure them from the piercing cold of December.

There was but little to interest the children this month in the garden or fields ; for with the exception of a few fine days, the weather was cold and gloomy ; the verdure of the meadows faded, the flowers perished, and the trees were stripped of their foliage. This cheerless state of nature suggested to Margaret's mind the following well known

LINES

Suggested by the sight of some late Autumnal Flowers.

1. These few pale autumn flowers,
     How beautiful they are !
   Than all that went before,
   Than all the summer store,
     How lovelier far ?

2. And why ? They are the last !
     The last ! the last ! the last !
   O ! by that little word
   How many thoughts are stirred ;
     That sister of the past !

3. Pale flowers ! pale perishing flowers !
     Ye 're types of precious things ;
   Types of those better moments
   That flit like life's enjoyments,
     On rapid, rapid wings.

4. Last hours with parting dear ones,
    (That time the fastest spends,)
   Last tears in silence shed,
   Last words half uttered,
       Last looks of dying friends.

5. Who, but would fain compress
       A life into a day,
   The last day spent with one
   Who, ere the morning's sun,
       Must leave us, and for aye?

6. O! precious, precious moments!
       Pale flowers! ye 're types of those
   The saddest, sweetest, dearest,
   Because, like those, the nearest
       To an eternal close.

7. Pale flowers! pale perishing flowers!
       I woo your gentle breath, —
   I leave the summer rose
   For younger blithesome brows; —
       Tell me of change and death!

Henry brought into the house a branch of
the Witch Hazel, which excited their curiosity,
not so much on account of the beauty of its yellow flowers which ornament its naked stems,
but that they should appear at this late period,
a solitary exception to the general desolation
by which it is surrounded.

Margaret. What has given it the name of
Witch Hazel?

Henry. I suppose on account of its being used by some simple, ignorant men, to discover springs of water, and mines.

M. How is it used?

H. I cannot tell you exactly; but I have heard it said, that those who make such pretensions, repair to the spot with a rod of it, which they hold in their hands in a peculiar manner, and that the rod will turn, and point to the spring or mine, if there be any in the neighborhood. Many a gaping, wondering spectator has been cheated, and deceived, and disappointed at last by these men, in whose hands the Witch Hazel is said to display its power.

M. Do you suppose a spring, or a mine, was ever discovered by this means?

H. No, never! it is all nonsense. I trust this part of the world has become so enlightened, that none but very ignorant people, will now be imposed upon by these jugglers.

DECEMBER.

Margaret. Look, brother, it begins to snow. How sorry I am that winter is coming again; we shall see no more flowers till its reign is over. Do you not wish that we could have winter without snow?

Henry. No; I do not. What do you suppose would be the consequence, if there was to be no snow?

M. I suppose it would be better for the plants, not to have so cold a covering over them.

H. You surprise me; have you forgotten the beautiful language with which David describes the snow? I will repeat what he says about the snow and cold.

"*He giveth snow like wool; he scattereth the hoar frost like ashes.*

"*He casteth forth his ice like morsels; who can stand before his cold.*" . . . . . .

"He giveth snow like *wool*." What do you suppose he meant by that?

M. That it was white like wool.

H. I apprehend he meant something else; that it afforded a warm covering like wool to the earth, and its many plants, without which they would have perished from the piercing cold.

M. It is a new idea to me; from appearances, I should suppose it far otherwise.

H. Snow is of great use to the vegetable kingdom, and in it we may see the wisdom of God; for without this protection, many roots would perish.

M. I spoke hastily about the snow; I see that if all our foolish wishes were gratified, confusion would soon be introduced into the works of our Heavenly Father. Let us be thankful that he moderates the continuance of the winter, and renders it useful to the earth; let us bless him if abundance of all things needful renders us free from the miseries which many suffer during this inclement season; and let us learn to contribute liberally to their relief. Let us also expect from his power things impracticable to all others.

H. It is wrong for us ever to feel dissatisfied with any of the changes of the seasons; for God at the creation pronounced everything he had done " VERY GOOD."

M. Winter, to be sure, seems at first thought to be cheerless; but when we come to think a little more about it, and remember how pleasantly our last winter was spent, and how many delightful evenings we enjoyed in conversation and books at our cheerful fireside, in company with our dear parents, and how comfortable it is to sit by a good fire when the storm is raging without, I can witness its approach with pleasure.

H. Had we a perpetual summer and a continued succession of flowers, we should perhaps soon become indifferent, and esteem them of little value; but now, after we have been sated with them, as it were, they are taken from us and laid aside for the present, that we may enjoy new pleasures, and be prepared to enjoy them with a keener relish when spring again bursts upon us.

NOTE.—Page 41.

" The amiable and indefatigable ornithologist, Alexander Wilson, who perhaps was better acquainted with the habits of our birds than any other person, when speaking of the *Sturnus predatorius*, or red winged black-bird, which, by the way, is by our farmers considered the most mischievous of birds, says 'their food in spring and the early part of summer consists of grub-worms, caterpillars, and various other larvæ, the silent but deadly enemies of all vegetation, and whose secret and insidious attacks are more to be dreaded by the husbandman than the combined forces of the whole feathered tribes together; for these vermin the black-birds search with great diligence; in the ground at the roots of plants, in orchards and meadows, as well as among buds, leaves and blossoms; and from their known voracity, the multitudes of these insects which they destroy must be immense.'

" Let me illustrate this by a short computation. If we suppose each bird, on an average, to devour fifty of these larvæ in a day, (a very moderate allowance) a single pair in four months, the usual time such food is sought after, will consume upwards of *twelve thousand*. It is believed that not less than a million pairs of these birds are distributed over the whole extent of the United States in summer; whose food being nearly the same, would swell the amount of vermin destroyed to *twelve thousand millions*. But the number of young birds may be fairly estimated at double that of their parents, and as these are constantly fed on larvæ for at least three weeks, making only the same allowance for them as the old ones, their share would amount to *four thousand two hundred millions*; making a grand total of *sixteen thousand two hundred millions* of noxious insects destroyed in the space of four months by this single species. The combined ravages of such a hideous host of vermin would be sufficient to spread famine and desolation over a wide extent of the richest and best cultivated country on earth.

"All this, it may be said, is mere supposition. It is, however, supposition founded on known and acknowledged facts.

"Mr Bradley, in his General Treatise on Husbandry and Gardening, shows 'that a pair of sparrows, during the time they have their young ones to feed, destroy on an average, (every week) about *three thousand three hundred and sixty* caterpillars.' This calculation he founded on actual observation. And it is well known that several kinds of our birds, such as the *Hirundo, muscicapa* genera, and some others, feed entirely on insects.

"I am fully persuaded, as long as farmers and others permit boys to roam over their fields and shoot down every small bird they meet — as long as young men are in the habit, on our anniversaries, of forming themselves into shooting parties, for the purpose of destroying small birds, which they do in immense numbers — I say as long as this wanton destruction of birds is carried on, we must expect innumerable hosts of noxious insects will continue to commit depredations on our orchards, our fields, and our gardens." — *New England Farmer, Vol.* vii. *No.* 1.